You Have t

It's Getting Better

You Have to Admit It's Getting Better

From Economic Prosperity to Environmental Quality

Edited by

Terry L. Anderson

HOOVER INSTITUTION PRESS
Stanford University   Stanford, California

www.hoover.org

Hoover Institution Press Publication No. 525

First printing 2004
10 09 08 07 06 05 04   9 8 7 6 5 4 3 2 1

Manufactured in the United States of America

The paper used in this publication meets the minimum requirements
of American National Standard for Information Sciences—Permanence
of Paper for Printed Library Materials, ANSI Z39.48-1992. ♾

Library of Congress Cataloging-in-Publication Data
You have to admit it's getting better : from economic prosperity to
environmental quality / edited by Terry L. Anderson.
      p.   cm. — (Hoover Institution Press publication ; no. 525)
   Includes bibliographical references and index.
   ISBN 0-8179-4482-6 (alk. paper)
   1. Sustainable development. 2. Economic policy. 3. Free
enterprise. 4. Right of property. 5. Population—Economic aspects.
I. Anderson, Terry Lee, 1946–   II. Series.
HD75.6.Y677 2004
338.9'27—dc22   2004003189

Contents

Tables and Figures

Figures

Acknowledgments

I first started reading Julian Simon's work in the 1980s and had the good fortune of meeting him at a conference sponsored by PERC, the Property and Environment Research Center, in the late 1980s. One might infer from his writings that he was a heartless economist interested only in debunking environmental myths and measuring economic scarcity. But nothing could be farther from reality. Julian Simon was a kind, gentle man who cared deeply about humanity and the individuals who comprise it. We all owe a debt of thanks to him for his unabiding faith in human beings as "the ultimate resource."

We also owe a debt of gratitude to Bjørn Lomborg for resurrecting the Simon tradition even if his original intent was to show how Simon was wrong. Unlike so many scholars, Lomborg is a true scientist, willing to test his hypotheses against the data and reject them if they prove to be false. Like Simon, Lomborg cares about humanity and the environment in which it lives. Also like Simon, Lomborg's optimism is contagious.

After Simon passed away, my colleagues and I at PERC were concerned that the tradition of his scholarship might not be maintained.

To encourage this scholarship, we approached the D & D Foundation for support of Julian Simon fellowships at PERC. Through support from the D & D Foundation, PERC has enjoyed hosting Julian Simon Fellows since 2000. The scholarship of five of those fellows—B. Delworth Gardner, Indur M. Goklany, Robert E. McCormick, Seth W. Norton, and Bruce Yandle—is featured in this volume. Without the D & D Foundation's investment in this scholarship, these ideas would not have been nurtured.

The Hoover Institution, where I am privileged to be a senior fellow, plays an important role in fostering these ideas. The institution produces "ideas defining a free society," and this volume is offered in that tradition. John Raisian, director, fosters an environment for scholars to conduct research and publish their findings, and without his support I could not have pursued this project. Marty and Illie Anderson have provided financial support for my position as the Marty and Illie Anderson Senior Fellow. As readers of this volume will note, property rights and the rule of law are indispensable to environmental quality. The Hoover Institution's property rights initiative, support by Peter and Kirsten Bedford, has raised our awareness of this link.

I personally owe a debt of gratitude to the authors of this volume, who have put up with my tardiness in bringing the publication to print, to my assistant at PERC, Michelle Johnson, who has made me more efficient than I would otherwise be. These are the really important members of the team that made this volume possible.

Contributors

Terry L. Anderson is the Martin and Illie Anderson Senior Fellow at the Hoover Institution, Stanford University, and the executive director of PERC—the Property and Environment Research Center, in Bozeman, Montana.

Madhusudan Bhattarai is a postdoctoral economist at the International Water Management Institute in Colombo, Sri Lanka.

B. Delworth Gardner is professor emeritus of economics at Brigham Young University; professor emeritus of agricultural economics at the University of California, Davis; and a 2002 PERC Julian Simon Fellow.

Indur M. Goklany was PERC's 2000 Julian Simon Fellow. He holds a Ph.D. in electrical engineering and has more than twenty-five years' experience addressing science and policy aspects of environmental and natural resource policy issues in state and federal government and in the private sector. He was formerly chief of the technical assessment division of the National Commission on Air Quality and a consultant in the Office of Policy, Planning, and Evaluation at the U.S. Environmental Protection Agency.

Bjørn Lomborg is director of the Institut for Miljøvurdering/Environmental Assessment Institute in Copenhagen, Denmark.

Robert E. McCormick is professor and BB&T Scholar in the John E. Walker department of economics at Clemson University and a senior associate at PERC.

Seth W. Norton is Aldeen Professor of Business at Wheaton College and a 2001 PERC Julian Simon Fellow. He holds a B.A. in history from Northwestern University and an M.B.A. in finance and a Ph.D. in economics from the University of Chicago.

Maya Vijayaraghavan is an economist with the Global Measles Branch, Global Immunization Division, National Immunization Program at the Centers for Disease Control and Prevention.

Bruce Yandle is professor emeritus of economics at Clemson University and a PERC senior associate.

Introduction

Property Rights and Sustainable Development

Terry L. Anderson

PIONEERING WORK BY the late Julian Simon brought the simple concept of scarcity to the forefront of environmental debates and focused attention on prices as an objective measure of that scarcity. His debates with environmentalists, policy analysts, and scientists were legendary because he challenged them to provide data to support their conclusions that the plight of human beings and the natural environment in which they live were getting worse.

Bjørn Lomborg rose to Simon's challenge and rejuvenated the debate over whether gloom-and-doom environmental predictions are supported by the evidence. As a statistician, Lomborg took seriously his job of testing the hypotheses that resources are becoming more scarce and the environment is getting worse. As he explains in the introduction to his book, he set out to show that Simon's optimistic conclusions were wrong and the belief that we have not been running out of natural

Terry L. Anderson is the executive director of PERC—the Property and Environmental Research Center, a think tank focusing on market solutions to environmental problems; a senior fellow at the Hoover Institution, Stanford University; and professor emeritus at Montana State University.

resources was wrong, but instead concluded that "children born today—in both the industrialized world and developing countries—will live longer and be healthier, they will get more food, a better education, a higher standard of living, more leisure time, and far more possibilities—without the global environment being destroyed. And that is a beautiful world" (Lomborg 2001, 352).

Julian Simon continually drove home the point that his findings and predictions, now buttressed by Lomborg's work, result from human ingenuity responding to impending scarcity and developing alternative technologies that mitigate against that scarcity. The key, of course, to mitigating natural resource constraints is to switch on human ingenuity, which allows us to accomplish more with a given amount of resources—in other words, to enjoy economic growth spurred by increased productivity from scarce resources. Since the fall of the Berlin Wall and communism, it has been clear that switching on this ingenuity requires getting the incentives right using the appropriate institutions. As we shall see, these institutions include property rights, the rules of law, and limited government. With these in place, economic growth will follow.

The doomsayers contend that such growth will ultimately deplete natural resources and destroy the environment, but Lomborg finds positive correlations between economic growth and environmental quality. He correlates the World Bank's environmental sustainability index with gross domestic product per capita across 117 nations, concluding that "higher income in general is correlated with *higher* environmental sustainability" (Lomborg 2001, 32). This idea is known as the "environmental Kuznets curve," based on Nobel laureate Simon Kuznets's earlier work on patterns of economic growth. Measuring environmental quality (for example, air quality) on the vertical axis and economic performance (for example, the gross domestic product, or GDP) on the horizontal axis, the relationship displays a J-curve. At lower levels of income, environmental quality can deteriorate as people trade environmental quality for economic growth. But as Bruce Yandle, Maya

Vijayaraghavan, and Madhusudan Bhattarai review in Chapter 3, all studies show that the relationship between environmental quality and economic performance becomes positive at higher levels of income because environmental quality is what economists call an *income-elastic good*. In other words, if income rises 10 percent, the demand for environmental quality rises more than 10 percent. Generally, the (annual) income level at which the turning point occurs is between $4,000 and $8,000, with the demand for water quality turning upward at lower levels of income than the income levels at which the demand for endangered species preservation turns upward.

In his pioneering data on carbon emissions, presented in Chapter 6, Robert McCormick estimates that net carbon emissions also appear to fit the J-curve, though the turning point occurs at much higher levels of income. McCormick admits that higher-income countries emit more carbon dioxide and other greenhouse gases into the atmosphere, but points out that wealthy countries also sequester more carbon through landfills, better farming techniques, and less burning of wood products, thus their net emissions of greenhouse gases ultimately decline.

The work of Indur Goklany in Chapter 2 adds further optimism to the potential for economic growth to be a driving force in improving environmental quality. Goklany estimates how the turning point for the J-curve shifts over time, given that new environmentally enhancing technologies are exported from rich countries to poor countries. For example, once a country such as the United States invents filters for water purification, developing countries do not have to "reinvent the wheel"; they can simply acquire the new filtering technology and improve water quality at lower levels of income. In case after case, Goklany shows that we can enjoy a given level of environmental quality measured by such considerations as access to clean water or clean air at lower income levels or we can enjoy higher levels of environmental quality at a given level of income. In short, economic growth allows the developing world to enjoy better living standards sooner than the developing world did in the past.

Missing from much of Simon's and Lomborg's type of data analysis is a good explanation of why improved environmental quality is positively correlated with economic growth and under what conditions will the progress shown by these data continue indefinitely into the future. Put in the popular vernacular of today, are the improvements found by Simon, Lomborg, and others sustainable and, if they are, under what circumstances?

It's the Institutions, Stupid

When the Eastern Bloc countries were freed of the shackles of communism, Milton Friedman said, "Privatize, privatize, privatize" (Friedman 2002, xvii). The assumption was that free-market discipline is all that is required for an economy to grow and develop and for growth to take off. Friedman believed that less developed countries, like those in the Eastern Bloc where both growth and environmental quality were at levels well below those in the developed Western nations, would only need to institute free-market reforms (privatization, fiscal and monetary discipline, open markets) to enjoy prosperity.

After more than a decade of experiments and a growing amount of data on what it takes to stimulate economic growth, however, Friedman has modified his position. Now he says: "It turns out that the rule of law is probably more basic than privatization. Privatization is meaningless if you don't have the rule of law. What does it mean to privatize if you do not have security of property, if you can't use property as you want to?" (Friedman 2002, xviii). Without the rule of law and secure property rights, growth is unlikely to occur. Free market discipline may be necessary for economic growth, but there is growing evidence that markets must be prefaced by the rule of law and secure property rights.

This does not mean that markets are not part of the equation for environmental quality. In fact, as B. Delworth Gardner describes in Chapter 4, criticisms of globalization and of freer international trade are unfounded. Contrary to popular opinion, trade liberalization is critical to improving human health and well-being and is more likely to improve environmental quality than reduce it.

Seth Norton actually calculates the statistical relationship between various freedom indexes and environmental improvements and reports his results in Chapter 5. His findings are supported by other scholars. For example, Panayotou (1997) tested five indicators of general institutional quality: respect/enforcement of contracts, efficiency of the bureaucracy, efficacy of the rule of law, extent of government corruption, and the risk of appropriation. He found that higher indexes for the institutional variables led to significant environmental quality improvements. In another study, Bhattarai (2000) found that civil and political liberties, the rule of law, the quality and corruption levels of government, and the security of property rights were important in explaining deforestation rates in sixty-six countries across Latin America, Asia, and Africa. Without question, institutions—especially those of property rights and the rule of law—are key to environmental improvements.

Sustainable Institutions

This strong empirical evidence helps to make operational the concept of sustainable development. The popular, though vague, term is used to argue that resource use today should leave future generations at least as well off as current generations. The notion of sustainability received its credibility in the environmental literature with publication of the *Blueprint for a Green Economy* in 1989. According to this book, sustainability means "that real incomes rise, that educational standards increase, that the health of the nation improves, that the general quality of life is advanced" (Pearce, Markandya, and Barbier 1989, 2).

By these standards, Lomborg's data and the data presented in this volume provide strong evidence that sustainable growth is occurring. Resource stocks are not declining and in many instances are actually growing as we discover new sources for existing resources and new ways of more efficiently using existing stocks. For example, soil resources are increasing as agricultural yields on rice, corn, and wheat have increased for decades, despite neo-Malthusian predictions to the contrary. Reserves of oil, natural gas, and coal continue to increase. Stocks of aluminum, zinc, iron, and copper, even with maintained use in society, have been steadily increasing for decades as technology develops more conservative production techniques and the price mechanism encourages exploration and new discoveries of underground reserves. As Lomborg concludes in his book, "All indicators seem to suggest that we are not likely to experience any significant scarcity of raw materials in the future" (Lomborg 2001, 148). In other words, the prosperity and improved human well-being that we are enjoying today are not leaving future generations worse off; rather, today's bounty is leaving them with more capital and larger stocks of natural resources.

This stands in sharp contrast to the undying conclusion of the doomsayers for whom the environment and the plight of human beings will always be getting worse. Paul and Anne Ehrlich (1996, 11) are perhaps the gloomiest.

> Humanity is now facing a sort of slow-motion environmental Dunkirk. It remains to be seen whether civilization can avoid the perilous trap it has set for itself. Unlike the troops crowding the beach at Dunkirk, civilization's fate is in its own hands; no miraculous last-minute rescue is in the cards. . . . [E]ven if humanity manages to extricate itself, it is likely that environmental events will be defining ones for our grandchildren's generation—and those events could dwarf World War II in magnitude.

Put a little less dramatically, respected Harvard biologist Edward O. Wilson contends that "the wealth of the world, if measured by domestic product and per-capita consumption, is rising. But if calculated from the condition of the biosphere, it is falling" (2003, 42).

In the past, such gloom and doom would have been followed with the traditional litany of environmental problems identified by Lomborg, but now there is a new Litany. The change is partly because of the growing amount of data such as those found by Simon and Lomborg and partly because of the loss of the bet that Paul Ehrlich made with the late Julian Simon. In that bet, Simon challenged Ehrlich to put his money where his mouth was by picking any five commodities and betting that they would rise in price between 1980 and 1990. Simon's point was that Ehrlich's gloom-and-doom model predicting exponential scarcity predicts rising prices, whereas Simon's human ingenuity model predicts falling prices. The wager allowed Ehrlich to pick five metals (he chose chromium, nickel, tungsten, copper, and tin) and hypothetically purchase $200 worth of each at the 1980 price for a total of $1,000. If the real prices went up over the ten-year period, Simon was to pay Ehrlich the difference between the initial and ending value of the hypothetical bundle of commodities; if they went down, Ehrlich was to pay Simon. In fact, all five declined in both nominal and real terms—Ehrlich had to pay Simon more than $400.[1]

In response, Ehrlich and his colleague Stephen Schneider challenged Simon to bet another $1,000, with a new Litany of gloomy predictions that would come to pass by 2004. That Litany included, to mention a few,[2]

- rising global temperatures.

- increased carbon dioxide in the atmosphere.

- more sulfur dioxide in the atmosphere in Asia.

- less firewood available per person in developing nations.

- significantly less land area covered by virgin tropical moist forest in 2004 than in 1994.

Simon refused the wager on the grounds that the new Litany did not measure human welfare, which is what Simon always contended was getting better. To the doomsayers, however, measures such as life expectancy, one of Simon's favorites, are "determined by a complex interaction of many factors, including infant and child nutrition, availability and sophistication of medical services, cleanliness of air and water, and other elements of environmental quality" (Ehrlich and Ehrlich 1996, 103).

Indeed, this is precisely the point of the chapters in this volume, of Lomborg's book, and of all of Simon's books: Measuring specific natural resource quantities or qualities tells us little about the plight of humanity because that plight is a complex mix. In the real world, the beach at Dunkirk is not a unidimensional plot of sand; rather, it includes boats, planes, food, and medical supplies, which are in a continual state of change because of human ingenuity, to say nothing of changes in political institutions.

As the authors in this volume show, especially important to the complex world are the property institutions that determine our incentives to husband natural resources and promote economic growth. Simon's confident, cheery predictions about human welfare emanated from his understanding of this complexity and of the potential for legal institutions to foster market processes that can coordinate the diffuse and complex information regarding resource scarcity and human demands.

Professor Robert Solow is one of the few economists who has tried to provide a conceptual context for considering this problem. Solow argues that sustainability "must amount to an injunction to preserve productive capacity for the indefinite future." This requires creating and maintaining "a generalized capacity to produce economic well-being" (Solow 1992, 14). He goes on to say that

> a sustainable path for the economy is thus not necessarily one that conserves every single thing or any single thing. It is one that replaces whatever it takes from its inherited natural and produced environment, its material and intellectual endowment. What matters is not the particular form that the replacement takes, but only its capacity to produce the things that posterity will enjoy. Those depletions and investment decisions are the proper focus. (15)

In other words, focusing on conservation of finite resources is not necessarily the path to sustainability, for two reasons. First, focusing on finite resources ignores the fact that our knowledge is limited. What we know about the availability of finite resources is limited by our willingness to invest time and money into finding those resources, and that time and money could be doing other things to improve well-being. There is a finite quantity of oil at any point in time because we are not willing to invest more in finding new reserves until scarcity of existing reserves makes it worth finding new inventories. Just as a supermarket only has a finite quantity of flour at a point in time because there is a cost of maintaining the inventory (storage, spoilage, and so on), so, too, is there a cost of finding oil reserves and maintaining ownership of those reserves until they are pumped. Seen in this light, it is not surprising that known oil reserves are continually rising despite the fact that we consume more of them all the time (Lomborg 2001, 124). Second, finite resources can be converted to other types of capital that have a greater ability to foster both intragenerational and intergenerational equity. For example, converting finite reserves of oil into plastic for medical treatment has the potential to provide services for posterity and is certainly the type of "replacement" that Solow had in mind.

With the focus on decisions rather than finite resource stocks, sustainability requires consideration of the institutions that create the incentive structure for human ingenuity. This incentive structure must include secure property rights and the rule of law that encourage development, innovation, conservation, and discovery of new resources. Growth and increasing wealth, through these mechanisms, lead to environmental sustainability by raising the demand for environmental quality and by allowing supply to match demand by making the resources available for achieving environmental quality. Economic growth is not the antithesis of environmental quality: rather, the two go hand in hand—if the incentives are right.

Conclusion

In his book, *The Ultimate Resource 2* (1998), the late Julian Simon built the coffin in which neo-Malthusian ideas should be buried. Simon believed that the ultimate resource is human ingenuity. As he was fond of saying, "With every mouth comes two hands and a mind." Or in the words of Aaron Wildavsky, "[S]carcity has yet to win a race with creativity" (Chai and Swedlow 1998, 91). Both of these scholars understood that institutions' getting the incentives right and prices that signal the extent of scarcity are why scarcity always loses the race.

The optimism shown by these two scholars also permeates the chapters in this volume. After reading it, you will have to admit the environment is getting better, not worse. In fact, I was recently asked what environmental problem concerned me the most for future generations. After a few seconds of thought, I answered that there was none. This is not to say that we will not face environmental problems, but I am optimistic that human ingenuity will continue to hammer out the institutions of freedom—namely, property rights and the rule of law— and those institutions will provide the incentive for us to solve whatever environmental problems might arise.

The findings in this volume, which link economic growth and environmental quality through the institutions of free societies, should drive the final nail into the doomsday coffin. Doomsayers will profess—as they have since Thomas Malthus—that exponential growth and consumption will ultimately run up against resource limits. Though the present-day doomsayers' predictions are no more likely to be borne out than those of past doomsayers, their concerns will help keep us vigilant. The lesson of this book is that our exercise of vigilance should be focused on developing and protecting the institutions of freedom rather than on regulating human use of natural resources through political processes. With a focus on the former, we will be able to have our environmental cake and eat it, too.

Notes

1. For Ehrlich's explanation of why the bet was a flawed measure of his position, see Ehrlich and Ehrlich (1996, 101).
2. For the complete list, see Ehrlich and Ehrlich (1996, 101–3).

References

Bhatarrai, Madhusudan. 2000. The environmental Kuznets curve for deforestation in Latin America, Africa, and Asia: Macroeconomic and institutional perspectives. Ph.D. dissertation. Clemson (South Carolina) University.

Chai, Sun-Ki, and Brendon Swedlow. 1998. *Aaron Wildavsky: Culture and social theory.* New Brunswick, N.J.: Transaction Publishers.

Ehrlich, Paul R., and Anne H. Ehrlich. 1996. *Betrayal of science and reason: How anti-environment rhetoric threatens our future.* Washington, D.C.: Island Press.

Friedman, Milton. 2002. Economic freedom behind the scenes, preface to *Economic Freedom of the World: Annual Report 2002,* by James Gwartney, Robert Lawson, with Walter Park, Chris Edwards, Veronique de Rugy, and Smita Wagh. Vancouver, B.C.: The Fraser Institute. Online: http://www.cato.org/economicfreedom/2002/efw022Dintro.pdf.

Lomborg, Bjørn. 2001. *The skeptical environmentalist: Measuring the real state of the world.* Cambridge: Cambridge University Press.

Panayotou, Theodore. 1997. Demystifying the environmental Kuznets curve: Turning a black box into a policy tool. *Environment and Development Economics* 2: 465–84.

Pearce, David, Anil Markandya, and Edward B. Barbier, eds. 1989. *Blueprint for a green economy.* London: Earthscan.

Simon, Julian L. 1998. *The Ultimate Resource 2.* Princeton, N.J.: Princeton University Press.

Solow, Robert. 1992. *An almost practical step toward sustainability.* Washington, D.C.: Resources for the Future.

Wilson, Edward O. 2003. *The future of life.* New York: Vintage Books.

Chapter 1

The Skeptical Environmentalist

Bjørn Lomborg

IN THE SAME WAY that one can only be for peace and freedom and against hunger and destruction, it is impossible to be anything but for the environment. But this has given the environment debate a peculiar status. Over the past few decades, there has been an increasing fusion of truth and good intentions in the environmental debate (Poulsen 1998). Not only are we familiar with the Litany—that the environment is in poor shape and getting ever worse—we *know* that the Litany is true and that anyone who claims anything else must have disturbingly evil intentions.[1]

That is why I felt it was important to write a book like *The Skeptical Environmentalist* (2001). My motives for writing this book were neither evil nor covert. My understanding, in all simplicity, is that democracy functions better if everyone has access to the best possible information. It cannot be in the best interest of our society for debate about such a vital issue as the environment to be based more on myth than on truth.

In the course of this chapter, I summarize two major points of my

Bjørn Lomborg is an associate professor of statistics in the department of political science, University of Aarhus, Denmark.

book. One of the most important aspects of the book was to confront the environmental myths and the Litany with the reality expressed in empirical data and statistics. The first part of this chapter is centered around this same exercise. Many predictions and claims made by environmental organizations are dismissed, and I hope to give an impression of the argument in my book—that things are indeed getting better.

The second part of this chapter is a condensed version of the explanation provided in my book as to why the myths and the Litany have been able to grow so strong. In the last part of the chapter, I present and respond to some of the criticisms my book has received.

Environmental Reality and Myths

I attempted over the course of *The Skeptical Environmentalist* to describe the principal areas that stake out humankind's potentials, challenges, and problems in the past, the present, and the future. I challenged the usual conception of the collapse of ecosystems because this conception is simply not in keeping with reality.

I found that we are not running out of energy or natural resources. There will be more and more food per head of the world's population. Fewer and fewer people are starving. In 1900, we lived for an average of thirty years: today, we live for sixty-seven years. According to the United Nations, we reduced poverty more in the last fifty years than we did in the preceding 500 years, and it has been reduced in almost every country.

Although its size and future projections are rather unrealistically pessimistic, global warming is probably taking place—but the touted cure of early and radical fossil fuel cutbacks is way worse than the original affliction. Moreover, the total impact of global warming will not pose a devastating problem for our future. Nor will we lose 25 to 50 percent of all species in our lifetime. In fact, we are losing probably 0.7 percent. Acid rain does not kill the forests, and the air and water around us are becoming less and less polluted.

Mankind's lot has actually improved in terms of almost every measurable indicator. But note carefully what I am saying here: that by far the majority of indicators show that mankind's lot has vastly *improved*. This does *not* mean, however, that everything is good enough. The first statement refers to what the world looks like, whereas the second refers to what it ought to look like.[2]

While on lecture tours, I have discovered how vital it is to emphasize this distinction. Many people believe they can prove me wrong, for example, by pointing out that a lot of people are still starving: "How can you say that things are continuing to improve when 18 percent of all people in the developing world are still starving?" The point is that ever fewer people in the world are starving. In 1970, 35 percent of the people in developing countries were starving. In 1996, the figure was 18 percent, and the United Nations expects that the figure will have fallen to 12 percent by 2010 (FAO 1996: I, Table 3; FAO 1999b, 29). This is remarkable progress: 237 million fewer people starving. Two billion more people are getting enough to eat today than in 1970.

The food situation has vastly improved, but in 2010, there will still be 680 million people starving, which is obviously not good enough. The distinction is essential—when things are not going well enough, we can sketch out a vision. And in this case, the vision is that fewer people must starve. This is our political aim. But if things are at least improving, then we know we are on the right track, although perhaps not at the right speed.

What Reality? The Use of References

Matter-of-fact discussion of the environment can be very difficult because everybody has such strong feelings on the issue. But at the same time, even as environmentalists, it is absolutely vital for us to be able to prioritize our efforts in many different fields—for example, health, education, infrastructure and defense—as well as the environment.

Over the course of the last few decades, we have developed a clear impression that the Litany is an adequate and true description of the world. We know that the environment is not in good shape. This is also why it has been possible for people to make erroneous claims, such as those mentioned in the previous pages, without needing to provide the evidence to authenticate them. For that reason, we also tend to be extremely skeptical toward anyone who says that the environment is not in such a bad state. To me, this indicates a natural and healthy reaction. And it's why I went to great lengths to document my claims.

I therefore included an unusually large number of notes in my book. In addition, I tried to source as much of the information from the Internet as possible. Thus, readers can go on to the Internet and download the relevant text to see from where I have retrieved my data and how I interpret that information. Of course, there will always be books and articles central to the relevant literature that are not available on the Internet.

I cannot overemphasize how important it is to me that there be no doubt about the credibility of my sources. For this reason, most of the statistics I used came from official sources that are widely accepted by the majority of people involved in the environment debate. Among these sources are agencies and programs of the Food and Agriculture Organization (FAO), the World Health Organization (WHO), the United Nations Development Programme (UNDP), and the United Nations Environment Programme (UNEP). Furthermore, I used figures published by international organizations such as World Bank and the International Monetary Fund (IMF), which primarily collate economic indicators.

Just because figures come from official international and national organizations does not, of course, mean that they are free from error—these figures often come from other publications that are less "official" in nature. It is therefore still possible to be critical of the sources of these data, but one does not need to worry to the same degree as one would were less-established sources used about the extent to which I simply present some selected results that are extremely debatable and that deviate from generally accepted knowledge. Focusing on official sources also means that I avoid one of the big problems of the Internet— that on this highly decentralized network you can find practically anything.

It is important to remember that the statistical material I presented in my book was usually identical to that used by the WWF, Greenpeace, and the Worldwatch Institute. People often ask where the "other" figures are, the ones these other organizations use, but there are no other figures. The figures I used are the official figures everybody uses.

When Lester Brown and I met in a television debate on the state of the world, one of the things we discussed was whether overall forest cover had increased or decreased since 1950. Brown's first reaction was that we should get hold of the FAO's *Production Yearbook*, which is the only work to include calculations of the area of forest cover from 1949 to 1994. This is the same book I had used as a reference, so we agreed on the standard. (In reality we were merely discussing who could look up a number correctly.)

Lester Brown believed there was less forest, whereas I thought there was more. I offered Lester Brown a bet, which he reluctantly declined and also which he would have lost. In 1950, the FAO estimated that the world had 40.24 million square kilometers of forest; in 1994, it estimated the world had 43.04 million square kilometers.

Confronting Myths with Reality

It is crucial to the discussion about the state of the world that we consider the fundamentals. This requires us to refer to long-term and global trends, considering their importance especially with regard to human welfare.

But it also is crucial that we cite figures and trends *that are true*. This demand may seem glaringly obvious, but unfortunately, the environment debate has been characterized by a tendency toward rather rash treatment of the truth. This is an expression of the fact that the Litany has pervaded the debate so deeply and for so long that blatantly false claims can be made again and again without any references and still be believed.

Take notice—this is not because of primary research in the environmental field which generally appears to be professionally competent and well balanced. It is because of the "knowledge" that is disseminated about the environment, which taps deeply into our doomsday beliefs. Such propaganda is presented by many environmental organizations—including the Worldwatch Institute, Greenpeace, and the WWF—and by many individual commentators, and it is readily picked up by the media. Let me stress that I am glad we have these organizations. They help point to problems that might otherwise be ignored. However, it should also be acknowledged that they represent certain interests, and as such, they present the public with one-sided information. My concern is the asymmetric flow of information that comes from trusting environmental organizations without the healthy critical angle one would normally put forward had the organizations been, for instance, business conglomerates.

Let us look at some of the more outstanding examples of environmental myth making.

Reality Check: Worldwatch Institute

Often the expressions of the Litany can be traced—either directly or indirectly—to the Worldwatch Institute. Its publications are almost overflowing with statements such as: "The key environmental indicators are increasingly negative. Forests are shrinking, water tables are falling, soils are eroding, wetlands are disappearing, fisheries are collapsing, rangelands are deteriorating, rivers are running dry, temperatures are rising, coral reefs are dying, and plant and animal species are disappearing" (Worldwatch Institute 1999a, 4). Powerful statements that make powerful reading—and they are made entirely without references.[4]

Discussing forests, the Worldwatch Institute states categorically that "the world's forest estate has declined significantly in both area and quality in recent decades" (Worldwatch Institute 1998a, 22).[5] As we previously saw, the decline in forests is simply not true. The longest data series from the FAO show that global forest cover has increased. Such global figures have not been referred to. Nor is reference made to figures regarding the forests' quality—simply because no such global figures exist.

Blatant errors are made with unfortunate frequency. Worldwatch Institute claims that "the soaring demand for paper is contributing to deforestation, particularly in the northern temperate zone. Canada is losing some 200,000 hectares of forest a year" (Worldwatch Institute 1998a, 9). Reference is made to the FAO's *State of the World's Forests 1997*, but if you refer to that source, you will see that in fact Canada added 174,600 hectares of forest each year (FAO 1997, 189).

In their 2000 overview, Worldwatch Institute lists the problems staked out in their very first *State of the World* publication (1984). Here is the complete list: "Record rates of population growth, soaring oil prices, debilitating levels of international debt, and extensive damage to forests from the new phenomenon of acid rain" (Worldwatch Institute 2000, xvii). The turn of the millennium would seem to be the natural point at which to take stock of the important issues, assess this list, ask if earlier problems have been overcome. However, Worldwatch Institute immediately tells us that we have not solved these problems. "Far from it. As we complete this seventeenth *State of the World* report, we are about to enter a new century having solved few of these problems and facing even more profound challenges to the future of the global economy. The bright promise of a new millennium is now clouded by unprecedented threats to humanity's future" (Worldwatch Institute 2000, xvii).

Worldwatch Institute does not return to look at the list but merely tells us that the problems have not been solved and that we have added even more problems since then. But does the Litany stand up if we check the data? The level of international debt may be the only place where we have not seen significant improvement: Although the level of debt declined steadily, the decline was slight, from 144 percent of exports in 1984 to 137 percent in 1999 (World Bank 2000a, 2000b).

Acid rain, although it harmed lakes, did very little, if any, damage to forests. Moreover, the sulfur emissions responsible for acid rain have declined in both Europe and the United States—in the European Union, emissions have decreased by a full 60 percent since 1980 (European Environment Agency 2000).

The soaring oil prices that cost the world a decade of slow growth from the 1970s into the mid-1980s declined throughout the 1990s to a price comparable with or lower than the pre–oil crisis price. Even though oil prices have almost doubled since the all-time low in mid-1998, a barrel price of $21.55 in 2001 is still way below the top price of $63 in the early 1980s. Moreover, most consider this spike is a short-term occurrence. The U.S. Energy Information Administration expects an almost steady oil price over the next twenty years at about $22–$24 a barrel (2002, 24–26).

Finally, speaking of record rates of population growth is just plain wrong—the record was set back in 1964 at 2.17 percent per year (U.S. Bureau of the Census 2000). Since that record, the population growth rate has been steadily declining, standing at 1.26 percent in 2000 and expected to drop below 1 percent in 2016. Even the absolute number of people added to the world peaked in 1990 with 87 million. The figure dropped to 76 million added in 2000 and is still decreasing.

Thus, in its shorthand appraisal of the state of the world since 1984, Worldwatch Institute sets out a list of problems, all of which have improved, all but one of which have improved immensely, and one of which is just plain wrong. Not a great score for sixteen years that have supposedly been meticulously covered by the Worldwatch reports. The problem, of course, is not lack of data—Worldwatch Institute publishes fine data collections, which are also used in my book—but merely a carelessness that comes with an ingrained belief in the Litany.

Reality Check: WWF

Toward the end of 1997, WWF focused on the Indonesian forest fires that were responsible for the thick clouds of smoke over much of Southeast Asia. There is no doubt that this was obnoxious for city dwellers, but WWF said the fires were a signal that the world's forests were "out of balance"—tidings that the Worldwatch Institute actually announced as one of the primary signs of ecological breakdown in 1997 (Worldwatch Institute 1998b, 15).

WWF proclaimed 1997 as "the year the world caught fire" because "in 1997, fire burned more forests than at any other time in history" (1997b, 1997c, 1998b). Summing up, WWF president Claude Martin stated unequivocally that "this is not just an emergency, it is a planetary disaster" (WWF 1997b). But on closer inspection, the figures do not substantiate this claim: 1997 was well below the record, and the only reason 1997 was the year when Indonesia's forest fires were noticed was because it was the first time they really irritated city dwellers. In all, Indonesia's forest fires affected approximately 1 percent of the nation's forests.

Also in 1997, WWF issued a press release entitled "Two-Thirds of the World's Forests Lost Forever" (1997d). In both this press release and its *Global Annual Forest Report 1997* (1997a, 1997d), WWF explained how its "new research . . . shows that almost two-thirds of the world's original forest cover has been lost." This seemed rather amazing to me, because most sources estimate about 20 percent.[6] I therefore called WWF in England and spoke to Rachel Thackray and Alison Lucas, who had been responsible for the press release, and asked to see the WWF research report on which that statement was based. All they were able to tell me, however, was that no report had ever existed and that the WWF had been given the figures by Mark Aldrich of the World

Conservation Monitoring Centre. Apparently, they had looked at some maximum figures and also, because of problems of definition, they had included the forests of the northern hemisphere in the original overview of forest cover, but not in the current one.[7]

From this nonreport, WWF (1997d) tells us: "[N]ow we have proof of the extent of forest already lost. . . . The frightening thing is that the pace of forest destruction has accelerated dramatically over the last five years and continues to rise." The United Nations, however, tells us that the rate of deforestation was 0.346 percent in the 1980s and just 0.32 percent from 1990 through 1995; not a dramatic increase in pace, but a decrease.[8]

WWF confides in us that nowhere is deforestation more manifest than in Brazil, which "still has the highest annual rate of forest loss in the world." In actual fact, the deforestation rate in Brazil is among the lowest as far as tropical forest goes; according to the United Nations, the deforestation rate is at 0.5 percent per year compared with an average of 0.7 percent per year (FAO 1997, 189).

In more recent material, WWF has lowered its estimate of original forest cover from 8,080 million hectares to 6,793 million hectares (about 16 percent) while increasing its estimate of the current forest cover from 3,044 million hectares to 3,410 million (about 12 percent), although this estimate is still about 100 million hectares lower than the U.N. estimate.[9] This means that WWF has lowered its estimates from 62.3 percent to 49.8 percent of the earth's forest that have been lost.[10]

This is still much more than the 20 percent commonly estimated. However, two independent researchers at the University of London and the University of Sussex (Fairhead and Leach 1998; Leach and Fairhead 1999) have tried to assess the sources and data used by WWF, the World Conservation Monitoring Centre (WCMC), and others in making such gloomy estimates of vast forest reductions. Considering the enormous amount of data, they have focused on the assessments of forest loss in West Africa, a place where WWF and the WCMC estimate a forest loss of 87 percent, or about 48.6 million hectares (Leach and

Fairhead 1999, 1). However, the documentation turns out to be based mainly on problematic bioclimatic forest zones, essentially comparing today's forests with where there may have been forests earlier. In general, the researchers find that "the statistics for forest loss in general circulation today massively exaggerate deforestation during the twentieth century" (Fairhead and Leach 1998, xix). The actual deforestation in West Africa is about 9.5 to 10.5 million hectares, or about five times less than what is estimated by WWF and the WCMC (Fairhead and Leach 1998, 183).

WWF (1999, 1) uses these forest estimates, among other measures, to make a so-called Living Planet Index, supposedly showing a decline of 30 percent over the past twenty-five years—"implying that the world has lost 30 percent of its natural wealth in the space of one generation." This index uses three measures: the extent of natural forests (without plantations), and two indices of changes in populations of selected marine and freshwater vertebrate species. The index is very problematic. First, excluding plantations ensures that the forest cover index will fall (because plantations are increasing), but it is unclear whether plantations are bad for nature overall. Plantations produce many of our forest goods, reducing pressure on other forests—in Argentina, 60 percent of all wood is produced in plantations that constitute just 2.2 percent of the total forest area, thus relieving the other 97.8 percent of the forests (FAO 1997, 13, Table 2). Although WWF states that plantations "make up large tracts of current forest area" (WWF 1998a, 6), they in fact constitute only 3 percent of the world's total forest area.[11]

Second, when using 102 selected marine species and 70 selected freshwater species, there is no way of ensuring that these species are representative of the innumerable other species. Indeed, because research is often conducted on species that are known to be in trouble, it is likely that such estimates will be grossly biased toward decline.

Third, in order to assess the state of the world, we need to look at many more and better measures. This is most clear when WWF (WWF

1998a, 24) actually quotes a new study that shows the total worth of the ecosystem to be $33 trillion annually (thus estimating the ecosystem to be worth more than the global production at $31 trillion). According to WWF (WWF 1998a, 24), it implies that the Living Planet Index's having dropped 30 percent means that we now get 30 percent less from the ecosystem each year or that we now lose some $11 trillion each year. Such a claim is almost nonsensical. Forest output has not decreased but increased—some 40 percent since 1970 (Worldwatch Institute 1999b, 77). And the overwhelming value of the ocean and coastal areas are in nutrient recycling, which the Living Planet Index does not measure at all. Also, marine food production has almost doubled since 1970. Thus, by their own measures, we have not experienced a fall in ecosystem services but actually a small increase.

In its *Living Planet Report 2002*, the WWF calculates a global footprint for the entire earth based on the area needed in six categories—cropland, grazing land, forests, fishing, infrastructure, and energy—to accommodate humankind's demand in a sustainable way. Based on its calculation, the WWF tells us that we need 1.2 Earths to satisfy our demand in a sustainable way and that if we do not change our current ways, we will be faced with a collapse in human welfare by 2030.

Energy consumption makes up for more than half of Earth's ecological footprint. How energy consumption can be translated into physical land area in any meaningful way constitutes a serious problem. The solution proposed by WWF is to calculate the area that needs to be covered with forests in order to soak up the carbon dioxide from fossil fuels. The consequence would be that with the current fossil fuel emissions, more than half of Earth's productive surface would be covered with forests—no wonder we are running out of space on paper. The strategy of raising forests to solve the carbon dioxide problem is but one solution—and it is the most space-intensive. By changing the focus away from forest sequestration to technologically feasible types of renewable energy, the ecological footprint is reduced by a factor of more than a hundred, leaving humankind with sustainable space in abundance (Danish Environmental Assessment Institute 2002, 35–38). Even the WWF has championed renewables for three decades—why are they not included in the calculation now?

The WWF also processes the much-inflated ecological footprint data in a computer model (the same infamous World3-model that was used to generate the flawed predictions in *Limits to Growth* from 1972) to estimate the costs that humankind might have to endure in the future. The model's projections reveal some surprisingly ominous costs for the mid-century generations: a global life expectancy age of 25, a global per-capita GDP equal to present-day Sudan, and a less-and-less-educated world. However, these predictions go against every future projection generated by official international institutes that unanimously conclude future generations are likely to be richer, healthier, and more equal. And a more thorough investigation of the dire predictions reveals that they have been generated using a model that excludes technological progress and human creativity and that the model contains an inherent mathematical tendency to overshoot and collapse (Danish Environmental Assessment Institute 2002, 22–33).

Reality Check: Greenpeace

In the Danish press, I pointed out that we had long been hearing figures for the extinction of the world's species that were far too high—including that we would lose about half of all species within a generation. The correct figure is closer to 0.7 percent in fifty years. This led to Niels Bredsdorff, the chairman of the Danish branch of Greenpeace, pointing out that Greenpeace had long accepted the figure of 0.7 percent. Notwithstanding, Greenpeace's official biodiversity report stated that "it is expected that half the earth's species are likely to disappear within the next seventy-five years."[12] Bredsdorff has never officially commented on this report, but he did manage to persuade Greenpeace International to pull the report off the Internet because it did not contain one single scientific reference.

Norwegian television confronted Greenpeace in Norway with this report. Four days later, having been more or less forced them into a corner, Greenpeace decided to hold a press conference, during which they raised all the general points I had mentioned, and they said that they were reevaluating their effort. The Norwegian daily *Verdens Gang* (March 19, 1998) reported:

> We have had problems adapting the environment movement to the new reality, says Kalle Hestvedt of Greenpeace. He believes the one-sided pessimism about the situation weakens environment organizations' credibility. Yet when most people do not feel that the world is about to fall off its hinges at any moment, they have problems taking the environmental organizations seriously, Hestvedt maintains.

By way of summary, a Greenpeace representative said that "the truth is that many environmental issues we fought for ten years back are as good as solved. Even so, the strategy continues to focus on the assumption that 'everything is going to hell'" (*Verdens Gang*, March 19, 1998).

Confronting Rhetoric and Poor Predictions

When we present an argument, there is never enough space or time to state all assumptions, include all data, and make all deductions. Thus, to a certain extent all argument relies on metaphors and rhetorical shortcuts. However, we must always be very careful not to let rhetoric cloud reality.

One of the main rhetorical shortcuts of the environmental movement is to pass off a temporary truism as an important indicator of decline. Try to see what your immediate experience is of the following quote from the Worldwatch Institute: "As a fixed area of arable land is divided among ever more people, it eventually shrinks to the point where people can no longer feed themselves" (2000, 7). This statement sounds like a correct prediction of problems to come. And yes, it is evidently true—there is a level (certainly a square inch or a speck of soil) below which we could not survive. But the important pieces of information are missing from Worldwatch's statement—we are not told what this level is, how close we are to it, and when we should expect to cross it.[13] Most people would probably be surprised to know that with artificial light each person can survive on a thirty-six-square-meter plot (forty-three square yards) and that companies produce commercially viable hydroponic food in even less space (Simon 1996, 100–101). Moreover, the FAO (2000b) finds in its newest analysis of food production to 2030 that "land for food production is seen to have become less scarce, not scarcer" (108). Thus the argument as stated is merely a rhetorical trick to make us think, "Oh yes, things must be getting worse."

This "rhetorical trick" has been used a lot by Worldwatch Institute. Talking about increasing grain yields, Lester Brown tells us that "there will eventually come a point in each country, with each grain, when the farmers will not be able to sustain the rise in yields" (1998a, 89) Again, this is obviously true, but the question is, how far away is the limit? This question remains unanswered while Brown goes on to conclude the somewhat unimaginative rerun of the metaphor: "Eventually the rise in grain yields will level off everywhere, but exactly when this will occur in each country is difficult to anticipate" (90). Likewise, Brown tells us that "if environmental degradation proceeds far enough, it will translate into economic instability in the form of rising food prices, which in turn will lead to political instability" (Brown 1996, 199–200). Again, the sequence is probably correct, but it hinges on the untold "if"—has environmental degradation actually proceeded that far? And that information is never demonstrated.

Greenpeace, in its assessment of the Gulf War, used similar rhetoric (1992, 8.1): "Any environment consists of many complex dynamic interactions, but the system will gradually, sometimes almost imperceptibly, break down once a threshold of damage has been passed. Whether this has happened in the Gulf only time will tell." Certainly it sounds ominous, but the important information of whether that threshold has been or is close to being crossed is left out.

Rhetoric, in various forms, is often employed. In one of the background documents for the U.N. assessment on water, the authors see two "particularly discomforting" alternatives for the arid, poor countries: "Either by suffering when the needs for water and water-dependent food cannot be met, manifested as famines, diseases and catastrophes. Or, in the opposite case, by adapting the demand to the available resources by importing food in exchange for other, less water-dependent products" (Falkenmark and Lundqvist 1997, 8). That sounds like a choice between the plague and cholera—until you think about it. Then you realize that they are essentially asking whether an arid country should choose starvation or partake in the global economy.

Worldwatch Institute wants us to change to renewable energy sources. Some of these arguments are entirely powered by rhetoric, as when they tell us: "From a millennial perspective, today's hydrocarbon-based civilization is but a brief interlude in human history" (1999a, 23). This is obviously true. A thousand years ago we did not use oil, and a thousand years from now we will probably be using solar, fusion, or technologies we have not yet thought of. The problem is that this does not really narrow down the point at which we have to change energy supply—now, in fifty years, in two hundred years? When seen from a millennial perspective, many things become brief interludes, such as the Hundred Years War, the Renaissance, the twentieth century, and indeed our own lives.

Likewise, when we argue about the consequences of ecosystem changes, it is easy to think of and mention only negative consequences. This is perhaps most evident when we discuss global warming and global climate change. Take, for instance, this description of climate change from *Newsweek*:

> There are ominous signs that the Earth's weather patterns have begun to change dramatically and that these changes may portend a drastic decline in food production—with serious political implications for just about every nation on Earth. The drop in food output could begin quite soon, perhaps only 10 years from now.

The evidence in support of these predictions has now begun to accumulate so massively that meteorologists are hard-pressed to keep up with it. In England, farmers have seen their growing season decline by about two weeks since 1950, with a resultant overall loss in grain production estimated at up to 100,000 tons annually. During the same time, the average temperature around the equator has risen by a fraction of a degree Celsius—a fraction that in some areas can mean drought and desolation. Last April, in the most devastating outbreak of tornadoes ever recorded, 148 twisters killed more than three hundred people and caused half a billion dollars' worth of damage in thirteen U.S. states.

To scientists, these seemingly disparate incidents represent the advance signs of fundamental changes in the world's weather. Meteorologists disagree about the cause and extent of the trend as well as over its specific impact on local weather conditions. But they are almost unanimous in the view that the trend will reduce agricultural productivity. (Gwynne 1975)

All this sounds familiar, like the greenhouse worries we hear today, but, surprisingly, it is actually an article from 1975 entitled "The Cooling World"—written during a time when we all worried about global cooling. Of course, our present worry about global warming is based on better arguments and more credible models. And because our societies were and are adjusted to the present temperature, a change, whether a cooling or a warming, will carry with it large costs.

But notice how *Newsweek*'s description conspicuously leaves out any positive consequences of cooling. Today, we worry that global warming will increase the outreach of malaria—consequently, a world believing in cooling should have appreciated the reduction of infected areas. Likewise, if we worried about a shortening of growing seasons with a cooling world, we should be glad that global warming will lengthen the growing season.[14] Obviously, more heat in the United States or the United Kingdom will cause more heat deaths, but it is seldom pointed out that this will be greatly outweighed by fewer cold deaths, which in the United States are about twice as frequent.[15] Notice, this argument does not challenge that total costs, certainly the total worldwide, from global warming will outweigh total benefits, but if we are to make informed decisions about solutions to global warming, we need to include both costs and benefits. If we focus only on the costs, it will lead to inefficient and biased decisions.

Another recurrent environmental metaphor is the likening of our current situation with that of Easter Island. A small island situated in the Pacific Ocean more than 1,900 miles west of Chile, Easter Island is most well-known for its more than 800 gigantic heads cut in volcanic stone, set all over the island. Archaeological evidence indicates that while producing the stunning statues, a thriving culture also began reducing the forests around A.D. 900. They used the trees for rolling the statues, as firewood, and as building materials. In 1400, the palm forest was entirely gone. Food production declined, statue production ceased in 1500, and, apparently, warfare and hunger reduced the population by 80 percent before an impoverished society was discovered in 1722 by Dutch ships (Brander and Taylor 1998).

Since then, Easter Island has been an irresistible image for the environmentalists, showcasing a society surpassing its limits and crashing devastatingly. A popular book on the environment uses Easter Island as its repeated starting point, even on the front cover (Gonick and Outwater 1996). Worldwatch Institute tells us in its millennium edition:

> As an isolated territory that could not turn elsewhere for sustenance once its own resources ran out, Easter Island presents a particularly stark picture of what can happen when a human economy expands in the face of limited resources. With the final closing of the remaining frontiers and the creation of a fully interconnected global economy, the human race as a whole has reached the kind of turning point that the Easter Islanders reached in the sixteenth century. (1999a, 11)

Isaac Asimov (Asimov and Pohl 1991, 140–41) merely tells us that "if we haven't done as badly as the extinct Easter Islanders, it is mainly because we have had more trees to destroy in the first place." Again, the problem is rhetoric that only indicates that crashing is indeed possible, but makes no effort to explain why such crashing should be likely. It is worth realizing that of the 10,000 Pacific islands, only twelve, including Easter Island, seem to have undergone declines or crashes, whereas most societies in the Pacific have indeed been prosperous (Brander and Taylor 1998, 122). Moreover, a model of Easter Island seems to indicate that its unique trajectory was due to a dependence on a particularly slow-growing palm tree, the Chilean wine palm, which takes forty to sixty years to mature (Brander and Taylor 1998, 129). This sets Easter Island apart from all the other Polynesian islands, where fast-growing coconut and Fiji fan palms make declines unlikely.

Moreover, the models predicting an ecological collapse need increasing populations with increasing need for resources to produce an overshoot. But in the modern world, such a scenario seems very unlikely, because increased wealth has caused a fertility decline (Brander and Taylor 1998, 135). And finally, it is worth pointing out that today's world is much less vulnerable, because trade and transport effectively act to reduce local risks.

The consequences of relying on rhetoric instead of sound analysis are many, primarily poor forecasts and the resulting biased decisions. Perhaps the most famous set of predictions came from the 1972 global bestseller *Limits to Growth*, which claimed we would run out of most resources. Indeed, gold was predicted to run out in 1981, silver and mercury in 1985, and zinc in 1990 (Meadows et al. 1972, 56). Needless to say, gold, silver, mercury, and zinc are still here, and most resources have actually become more abundant (Lomborg).

Let us end this section with two examples from one of America's foremost environmentalists, professor Paul Ehrlich, a prolific writer and discussant.

In 1970, as the first Earth Day approached, Ehrlich wrote an article in *The Progressive* styled as a fictitious report to the president of the United States and looking back from the year 2000. The fictitious report underlines how environmental scientists in the 1960s and 1970s had "repeatedly pointed out" that overcrowding, hunger and environmental deterioration would lead to "environmental and public health disasters" (25). Unfortunately, people had not heeded the warnings, and Ehrlich tells of a United States that is almost unrecognizable, with a severely decimated population at 22.6 million (8 percent of current population) and a diet of 2,400 daily calories per person (less than the current African average).[16] As an almost ironic glimmer of hope, Ehrlich does not expect that the United States is faced with any immediate limits-to-growth threat of running out of resources because of the "small population size and continued availability of salvageable materials in Los Angeles and other cities which have not been reoccupied" (24).

This view was fleshed out in the book *The End of Affluence*, written by Ehrlich with his wife Anne (Ehrlich and Ehrlich 1974). Here they worried about how global cooling would diminish agricultural output and forecast trouble with the fisheries, because the global catch had reached its maximum (28–30). They saw a society that was driven by deluded economists "entrapped in their own unnatural love for a grow-ing gross national product" (158). The ultimate consequence was clear: "It seems certain that energy shortages will be with us for the rest of the century, and that before 1985 mankind will enter a genuine age of scarcity in which many things besides energy will be in short supply. . . . Such diverse commodities as food, fresh water, copper, and paper will become increasingly difficult to obtain and thus much more expen-sive. . . . Starvation among people will be accompanied by starvation of industries for the materials they require" (33).

Though rhetorically eloquent, time has not been kind to these predictions. Thus, when we evaluate the data on the state of the world, it is important that we not be swayed by rhetoric or simplistic models and that we use and present the best indicators and the best models.

Summing Up

Many people have pointed out at lectures that although I may be right in claiming that things are not as bad as we thought they were, such arguments should not be voiced in public as they might cause us to take things a bit too easy. Although one can argue such a position, it is important to understand how antidemocratic such an attitude really is: We (the few and initiated) know the truth, but because general knowledge of the truth will cause people to behave "incorrectly," we should refrain from broadcasting it. Moreover, such a course of argument will also be harmful to the environmental movement in the long run since it will erode its most valuable asset, its credibility. I think that, in general, pretty strong arguments would have to be presented for it to be permissible to withhold the truth for the sake of some elitist, general good.

This does not mean that I am a demonic free-market individualist. I believe that there are many circumstances in which environmental intervention is necessary if we are to prevent unnecessary pollution and keep people from shunning their responsibilities. However, we should only intervene if it is reasonable to do so, not simply because myth and worry lead us to believe that things are going downhill.

Often we hear that environmental worry has been and is an important factor in getting action on cleaning up the environment, that essentially many of the global indicators go in the right direction because people worried in earlier times. However, this is often misleading, even incorrect. Air pollution in London has declined since the late nineteenth century, but the decline for most of the twentieth century has been mainly because of a change in infrastructure and fuel use and only slightly, if at all, because of environmental worries expressed in concrete policy changes. Moreover, even to the extent that worries have mattered in policy decisions, as they undoubtedly have during the past thirty years in, say, air pollution, this does not assure us that our resources could not have been put to better use.[17] To the extent that worries have prodded us to spend more money on the environment than we would have done if we'd had the best available information, the argument for environmental worries is a replay of the democratic dilemma above. Although kindling public concern clearly makes people choose more "correctly" as seen from an environmental viewpoint, it leads to an "incorrect" prioritization as seen from a democratic viewpoint because it skews the unbiased choice of the electorate.

In general we need to confront our myth of the economy under-cutting the environment.[18] We have grown to believe that we are faced with an inescapable choice between higher economic welfare and a greener environment.[19] But surprisingly, and as documented throughout my book, environmental development often stems from economic development—only when we get sufficiently rich can we afford the relative luxury of caring about the environment.

This also has implications for our discussions on prioritization. Many people love to say that we should have a pollution-free environment. This is a delightful thought, of course. It would be nice as well to have a country with no disease or the best possible education for all its young people. The reason this does not happen in real life is that the cost of getting rid of the final disease or educating the slowest student will always be ridiculously high. We invariably choose to prioritize in using our limited resources.

One American economist pointed out that when we do the dishes, we are aiming not to get them clean but to dilute the dirt to an acceptable degree (Simon 1996, 226–27). If we put a washed plate under an electron microscope we are bound to see lots of particles and greasy remnants. But we have better things to do than spend the whole day making sure that our plates are a little cleaner (and besides, we could never get them completely clean). We prioritize and choose to live with some specks of grease. Just how many specks we will accept depends on an individual evaluation of the advantages of using more time doing dishes versus having more leisure time. But the point is that we—in the real world—never ask for 100 percent.

Similarly, we have to find a level at which there is sufficiently little pollution such that our money, effort, and time are better spent solving other problems. This calls for access to the most accurate and thorough and least myth-based knowledge.

Why Do We Hear So Much Bad News?

In the vast majority of nations, people believe that the environment is worse "somewhere else" than in their own country. It is not unthinkable that the environmental problems we experience at a national and international level either are not localized or occur in sparsely populated areas. But it still points to the fact that our knowledge of things close to us, which is derived from our own experiences, is not the primary source of our fears for the environment. On the contrary, we seem more worried about conditions the further away from us they are, both physically and mentally.

This points to the fact that our fears for the environment are, to a high degree, communicated, and here I will look at three of the most important communicators: researchers, organizations, and the media. I will argue that there is good reason to believe that all three communicators will present us with a preponderance of negative tidings. And finally, comment should be passed on our own willingness to listen to and believe bad news.

Research

Research is basically a question of revealing truths about ourselves and our surroundings, be these manmade or natural. But research does not simply come about of its own accord; it has to be financed. This means that the problems to be investigated are influenced, to some degree, by the interests of those who finance the research.

In our modern society, much research is publicly funded, which means there will be certain expectations as to the relevance of the research to society.[20] There is nothing at all suspicious about this, as we probably expect to get a reasonable return on our tax money, but it does have consequences for the characteristics of the research.

Research basically has built-in lopsidedness. If a scientist says that she has investigated her field and not found any general problems, we as a society need do no more. If, on the other hand, the scientist investigates her field and finds a potentially momentous problem, it would be common sense to take action and at least research the field more thoroughly. This means that, other things being equal, we have research that tends to investigate areas in which problems can arise.

At the same time, another imperfection also exists. It is not always easy to identify exactly what constitutes a problem. If there have always been periodic oxygen shortages in the Gulf of Mexico, then the phenomenon is probably not a problem. But if occurrences have become more frequent because of an excess of nutrients, then the problem could well be serious. Identification of a problem depends on the theory by means of which we interpret what we observe in the world.

In this connection, a simple, easily comprehensible theory is fundamental: a theory that links human action (how we damage nature) and a clearly identifiable problem. At the same time, most environmental problems are incredibly complex, and it can be difficult to accept or reject a theory within a short period of time. Global warming, the eradication of species, and oxygen depletion are problems the causes and connections of which can only be determined over a long period and at great cost.

A situation with a potential problem and an easily explained theory will therefore attract sizable grants for more research, and we can expect this research to continue over long periods of time. There is nothing wrong with this situation per se. In reality, it is an indication of a well-functioning society: Many researchers look into many different problems, thereby providing us with the knowledge we need to make sure that only a very few problems ever develop into big ones.

We must expect that efficient research will provide information about many potential future problems. But hearing so many stories, as we do now, should not necessarily be taken as an indication that dooms-day is nigh. On the contrary.

Acid rain is a good example. In the late 1970s and early 1980s, there was a considerable loss of foliage in the forests of central Europe. This alone would probably have triggered considerable interest among researchers in the affected countries. However, German scientists also believed that they were able to link foliage loss to industrial pollution. They predicted that all forests exposed to acid rain would suffer substantial damage. This led to fears on a much wider scale, and national research programs were initiated throughout most of the Western World. This also presented the potential for a whole series of research projects. Some of Norway's foremost acid rain scientists wrote that "the possibility for reduced forest growth was the main reason why it was possible to get large funding for research on the effects of acidic rain" (Abrahamsen, Stuames, and Tveite 1994, 298). Ten years later all fears had evaporated—acid rain only damages trees under very rare conditions—but during these ten years we heard an incredible number of theories, partial research results, and popular—primarily negative—explanations.

All the same, it was still a good idea to investigate the connections. Had an unambiguous explanation been found, it would have provided us with the best premise for handling the potential problems. But in going ahead with the investigations, we also ought to prepare ourselves for hearing many a negative story—many of which will not necessarily turn out to be true.

Organizations

As further funding comes on tap, research becomes a veritable industry. Researchers begin to investigate subsidiary fields and special cases within the original problem field without necessarily having an interest in or any breadth of view of the field as a whole.

Although the field naturally retains its professional integrity, it gradually becomes increasingly difficult to challenge the consolidating problem. For one thing, a natural tendency to secure funding for their own special field will encourage scientists not to criticize the overall field of research. For another, many participants only investigate problems within the field and will not challenge the premises of the field. In this way, the field achieves a certain degree of independence and begins to define its own reality.

One critic of such institutionalization is retired professor Aksel Wiin-Nielsen, a former secretary-general of the U.N. World Meteorological Organization. On the question of global warming, he commented: "The most important explanation as to why so much extensive theoretical work in the development of climate models has been done during the last ten years is that the development of models sustains funding and secures jobs at research institutions."[21] Of course, criticism as far-reaching as this is extremely difficult to substantiate adequately, and the U.N. Intergovernmental Panel on Climate Change (IPCC) has criticized Wiin-Nielsen for his failure to do so.[22] My point is simply to stress that in important fields of research it can be difficult to present information that goes against institutional interests.

One researcher has argued in the esteemed journal *Energy Policy* that it was actually the climate researchers, together with, for example, the windmill manufacturers and environment bureaucracies, who were the primary political initiators of the climate negotiations (Boehmer-Christiansen 1997). In other words, it was institutionalized interests, not, as you may have thought, the prospect of possible global warming, that was behind the tremendous support for the carbon dioxide restrictions included in the Kyoto Protocol of December 1997.

But there also are other, more politically oriented organizations that disseminate environmental research. Such organizations include the obvious environmental movements such as Greenpeace, WWF, and the Worldwatch Institute, but also the more traditional organizations like the National Federation of Independent Business (NFIB) and the American Farm Bureau Federation (AFBF) in the United States[23] or the Confederation of British Industry and the National Farmers Union in the United Kingdom. All these organizations have vested interests in the political consequences and decisions that result from research. The NFIB and the AFBF have an interest in protecting their members, and they work to promote decisions that are to the advantage of their members. In the same way, environmental organizations base their activities on a desire to promote decisions that are good for their members.

The difference is that while the traditional organizations usually fight for traditional values, such as the distribution of time and money, the environmental organizations fight for bigger forests, diversity of species, restoration of natural environments, strict regulations of chemicals, and so on. Nevertheless, we can argue that the environmental organizations are fighting for the interests of their members because in the last analysis they are able to do only what their members, sympathizers, and supporters believe is good and necessary—because without their backing the organizations' campaigns would be more or less worthless. The organizations may present themselves as the patrons of the penguins and the pine trees, but they are dependent on people who sympathize with their points of view and contribute money, prestige, and influence through their democratic vote and pressure on the politicians.

Most people seem to be perfectly aware that when the NFIB tells us that an environmental regulation of industry is unnecessary, they may have good and sensible arguments, but they certainly also have a clear interest in avoiding such regulation. Many people tend to view the NFIB's arguments with a certain natural skepticism because they know that the argument could also be a cover for ulterior motives. This considered, it seems amazing that many people are not equally aware that the environmental organizations also have an interest in environmental regulation.[24] It may be that the environmental organizations have better arguments for regulation (but, of course, their arguments may also be poorer), but it ought to be obvious that they, too, have an interest in arguing toward a particular end.

Thus, just as the industry and farming organizations have an obvious interest in portraying the environment as just-fine and no-need-to-do-anything, so do the environmental organizations have a clear interest in telling us that the environment is in a bad state and that we need to act now. And the worse they can make this state appear, the easier it is for them to convince us we need to spend more money on the environment rather than on hospitals, kindergartens, and so on. Of course, if we were equally skeptical of both sorts of organizations, there would be less of a problem. But because we tend to view environmental organizations with much less skepticism, this might cause a grave bias in our understanding of the state of the world.

Note, however, that this is only a theoretical argument as to the environmental organizations' having an interest in portraying the world as gloom and doom. The extent to which they actually do so is one of the themes of my book, *The Skeptical Environmentalist*.

The Media

The media are our primary information source. They pass on the results of research, possibly helped along by the organizations. The media play a central role in this path of communication because the world has become so complex that we can no longer rely primarily on our own experiences. Instead, the mass media provide much of our understanding of reality.

But their particular way of providing us with news profoundly influences our view of the world. There is rarely much doubt that facts reported in an article or a news report are generally true. In that sense, the media simply reflect the world as it is. What is interesting, however, is the long and winding path between an event taking place in the world and its possible appearance and placement in the media. Looking at news reporting in this way shows how the media systematically present us with a lopsided version of reality: a picture of reality that is incoherent and sporadic, though at the same time reassuringly predictable and familiar; a picture in which problems fill every column and the emphasis is on drama and conflict. As an editor-in-chief has put it, "Producing a paper is a question of distorting proportions" (Bent Falbert, quoted in Meilby 1996, 53).

This media-based reality has numerous consequences. First, the incoherent information we are given provides us with too little knowledge of concrete problems to enable us to take part in a democratic decision-making process. Second, we feel sufficiently comfortable that we believe we *do* have sufficient knowledge to partake in the debate and to make valid decisions. Third, we will often get a far too negative and distorted impression of problems.

One consequence of the demand for rapid news delivery is that our view of the world becomes fragmented. Our demand for interesting and sensational news means that our picture of the world becomes distorted and negative. Coupled with problem-oriented research and the finely tuned public relations units of the environmental organizations, this can provide serious bias toward a negative appraisal of the state of the world.

Note, however, that it is not anybody's "fault." We get primarily negative news not because the journalists have evil intentions, but because the news media are placed in an incentive structure that makes it profitable to focus on negative occurrences. The environmental organizations are interest groups like all others, and they argue in favor of their own cause. That we primarily believe their negative news is not their fault, but ours, because we are only skeptical of the AFBF arguments and not of those from the environmental lobby. Research is mainly concerned with potential problems. This is socially beneficial because it gives us the best opportunity to handle problems in the future, but it also means that we are continuously faced with news of potential disasters.

We cannot change this negative lopsidedness. Instead, we must come to grips with the fact that the stream of information we receive is inherently lopsided and compensate for it. Unfortunately, this may be

very difficult because we inherently tend to think that things were better
in the old days and that everything is going in the wrong direction. The
Scottish philosopher David Hume wrote in 1754 that "the humour of
blaming the present, and admiring the past, is strongly rooted in human
nature, and has an influence even on persons endued with the profound-
est judgment and most extensive learning" ([1987], 464).

Sal Baron wrote in his book about the history of the Jews that
prophets who made optimistic predictions were automatically considered to be false prophets (quoted in Simon 1995, 19–24). An Assyrian
stone tablet, many thousands of years old, tells us of the obstinate feeling
of decline: "Our earth is degenerate in these latter days; bribery and
corruption are common; children no longer obey their parents; every
man wants to write a book, and the end of the world is evidently
approaching" (quoted in Simon 1996, 17). Moreover, it has been sug-
gested that the spirit of ascetic Calvinism still hovers over Western
civilization (Knudsen 1997): In a sense, when we have done so very
well, maybe we ought to be punished? In that light, the worry over global
warming could be seen as a search for a nemesis, to punish our overconsumption, a penalty for our playing the Sorcerer's Apprentice.

These observations seem to suggest that historically, and perhaps
biologically, we are disposed to welcome negative news. But if we are
to have a rational political-decision-making process and choose the best
means to the right objectives, we must bear in mind that the stream of
information we are receiving is unbalanced. We hear many negative and
problematic stories every day that should not necessarily be taken at
face value. Television networks try to attract attention, environmental
organizations argue for their causes, and research science already is
examining a variety of solutions to cover us if and when the problem
occurs.

Of course, this does not mean that we can just sit back and ignore
all problems. But it does imply that we must view the world with a
healthy portion of skepticism and take on the challenges because we

know that we are being confronted systematically with a surplus of negative news.

Criticism: Science Defending Itself Against the Skeptical Environmentalist?

The Skeptical Environmentalist spurred much controversy and debate. It was not surprising, albeit a little depressing, that several environmental pundits did not engage in a discussion of the substance of the book but instead engaged in a discussion of my person by questioning my motives. In this section, I will present and respond to some of the criticism that actually did engage a discussion of the book's facts. This type of criticism mainly stemmed from two prestigious scientific magazines, namely, the review of the book in *Nature* (Pimm, Stuart, and Harvey 2001) and the article series "Misleading Math About the Earth: Science Defends Itself Against *The Skeptical Environmentalist*," in *Scientific American* (January 2002). In both cases, I attempted to get a reply published in the magazines only to be denied the space. Five months later, I was allowed about a page in *Scientific American*. It was immediately followed by the editor's equally long condemnation of my letter.

The criticism focused on five major areas, which I will address one by one.

References

Much of the criticism focused on my use of references. In *Nature*, Pimm and Harvey carried out some statistics of my references in order to illustrate a bias toward secondary literature. They found that of the approximately 2,000 references (it's actually closer to 3,000), 5 percent come from news sources, 30 percent come from Web downloads and 1 percent are original papers in *Nature* (149). They concluded that my book relies heavily on secondary sources and nonpeer-reviewed material.

That 5 percent are from news sources is not surprising—the book was also trying to document what Greenpeace thinks about global warming, organic farmers about sperm quality, indeed, people in general about the environment in general. That 30 percent are from the Web says nothing—by far the majority is from the United Nations, World Bank, the Worldwatch Institute, the European Union, and so on, as I state clearly in the book. That Pimm and Harvey find it problematic that there are only 1 percent *Nature* articles seems somewhat strange— why should my book have referenced *Nature* articles more? Are *Science* articles not as good?

Scientific American also questioned my use of references. One of the authors, Stephen Schneider, wrote the following in the beginning of his article: "Before providing specifics of why I believe each of these assertions is fatally flawed, I should say something about Lomborg's methods. First, most of his nearly 3,000 citations are to secondary literature and media articles. Moreover, even when cited, the peer-reviewed articles come elliptically from those studies that support his rosy view that only the low end of the uncertainty ranges will be plausible" (2002).

I would argue that there is an important distinction between secondary sources and media articles. When discussing the entire state of the world, it would be incredibly inefficient not to use the vast collection of data and theory offered by secondary sources—this is exactly the reason for secondary literature and in general why it is possible to have specialization in science. However, almost all of these secondary sources are exactly the ones used by almost all discussants of the state of the world—U.N. agencies (the FAO, the UNDP, the UNEP, WHO, and so on), the IMF, World Bank, the Organisation for Economic Cooperation and Development, the World Resources Institute, the Worldwatch Institute, the European Union, and U.S. government agencies. Surely most people—including myself—would consider these reports the best available summary of our understanding of climate science, which was my argument for primarily using them as references.

Population Growth

One of the articles in the *Scientific American* series included a section that criticized my apparent lack of interest in demographic changes and population growth. In that section, John Bongaarts (Bongaarts 2002) challenges my contention that "the number of people is not the problem." As we will later see, it is symptomatic that my critics actually agree with me on my major points. This is also the case with Bongaarts, who starts off by writing that "people are living longer and healthier lives" and that "environmentalists who predicted widespread famine and blamed rapid population growth for many of the world's environmental, economic and social problems overstated their cases." However, he then goes on to challenge the more marginal arguments in my book.

Bongaarts claims that I use selective statistics to generate the impression that the population problem is a thing of the past. First, he neglects to write that when I say the number of people is not the problem, I then identify what is the problem: poverty. Second, I do not use selective statistics. Indeed, the ensuing documentation seems to point its accusing finger the other way. In his article, Bongaarts says that the global population growth rate has indeed declined slowly, but that absolute growth remains close to the top. I would say that the population growth rate has declined more than "slowly," as it has actually declined from 2.17 percent in 1964 to 1.26 percent today (a decline of more than 40 percent). Bongaarts's second claim, that the absolute growth remains close to the very high levels of the recent decades, is not convincing—the 76 million added today is the lowest number in the last two decades.

Although he accepts that the world would probably be able to feed the future population, Bongaarts fears that this might have severe environmental consequences (the Earth might turn into a "giant human feedlot") and accuses me of not dealing adequately with these problems. However, according to FAO (2000b) estimates, we are currently using about 11 percent of the Earth's land surface area for agriculture, and in 2030, when we will be feeding more than 8 billion people better than we are now (3,100 calories per person compared with a little more than 2,800 today), we will be using 12 percent—this would hardly turn "the Earth into a giant human feedlot." Moreover, had Bongaarts accessed the available statistics, he could have seen that the increase in agricultural land use was actually *greater* over the last twenty-five years than it is projected to be over the coming thirty years (105).

In the case of migration from rural to urban areas in the developing world, Bongaarts correctly cites me for considering this a welcome development because urban dwellers generally have higher standards of living than villagers. Bongaarts argues, however, that the flow of migrants is now so large that it overwhelms the absorptive capacity of the cities thus resulting in "health conditions in slums that are often as adverse as in rural areas." This makes Bongaarts conclude that the traditional urban advantage is eroding in the poorest countries—unfortunately, an unsubstantiated claim without any references. Where does this claim come from? It cannot be deduced from his previous thoughts on health in the slums compared with the rural areas. Such logic is flawed because it compares health conditions among the worst areas of the city (slums) with the average rural areas, a typical and incorrect comparison, as I point out in my book (Lomborg 2001, 49).

All in all, Bongaarts' criticism supported my major points, found no convincing examples of incorrect or selective data, and ended up discussing marginal issues based on his own conviction without backing up his statements with statistics.

Biodiversity

Both *Nature* and *Scientific American* criticized my chapter on biodiversity. In *Scientific American*, Thomas Lovejoy (2002) found it "disconcerting" that I had begun the biodiversity chapter with questioning whether biodiversity is important before discussing its size. I understand why this would be disconcerting to an environmental advocate or policy participant, but why would it be disconcerting to a scientist that we question the basis for our concern? Lovejoy seems to indicate that it should be obvious to any good man or woman that I am wrong, simply because I dare to ask the question.

When it comes to the substantial issues such as the rate of extinction, my book refutes both Norman Myers's (1979) assertion that 40,000 species are lost from the globe every year and the general application of Edward O. Wilson's rule of thumb, which claims that a 90 percent reduction in area would halve the number of species (Mann 1991, 737). Myers's figure of 40,000 species lost was not based on scientific research, and Wilson's theory—although based on empirical evidence—was developed in order to explain the number of species on islands. If the island gets smaller, the species will have nowhere to escape. However, the same is not the case in a mainland rain forest because many animals and plants can go on living in the surrounding areas. Empirical evidence suggests that this is exactly what they do; therefore, Wilson's rule of thumb could lead to a significant overestimate of the extinction rate. It seems that Lovejoy also used a "Myers estimate" in the *Global 2000 Report to the President of the U.S.: Entering the 21st Century*, wherein he predicted that 15 percent to 20 percent of all species would have vanished by 2000 (Barney 1980, II, 331). My chapter showed that, until recently, such estimates still provided the basis for environmental projections and press releases. It was therefore necessary to present the more likely prediction—based on detailed empirical evidence—that we probably are losing 0.7 percent of all species over the next fifty years. Assuming that the extinction of species presents humankind at least with an ethical predicament, the central point of my chapter on biodiversity was thus to present the reader with the right proposition of the problem. It is noteworthy that none of the critiques actually challenged this estimate. Instead the critiques more or less concentrated on minor arguments and field studies—presumably because if you cannot catch the big fish you should concentrate on the smaller.

One of the arguments was that Myers's estimate might have been off the mark but that "he deserves credit for being the first to say the number is large and for doing so at a time when it was difficult to make more accurate calculations" (Lovejoy 2002). Here Lovejoy essentially acknowledges that Myers did not have scientific basis for claiming that 40,000 species are lost every year, but nevertheless feels it was good that Myers said it. This is not how I understand good science.

In *Nature*, Pimm and Harvey found that the extinction rate of 0.7 percent over the next fifty years was "strikingly discordant with the 10–40 percent of well-known species that teeter on the brink of extinction" (2001, 149). However, the extinction rate and the percentage of species on the brink of extinction are two entirely different measures. Actually, an analysis of the 1,000 birds claimed to be teetering on extinction found that, primarily because of conservation efforts, "relatively few of these species are likely to become extinct by 2015" (Heywood and Stuart 1992, 28). Thus, merely contrasting the two numbers to imply that I am wrong in my biodiversity loss estimate is plainly an incorrect argument.

Another argument seems to be based on the typical environmental Litany: It might not have gone wrong yet but it will go wrong soon. In other words, the reason we do not see species becoming actually extinct in many areas despite a significant habitat loss is because the species are just barely hanging on, essentially as "living dead." This should apparently explain that even though the Brazilian Atlantic rain forest has been cut down by about 90 percent, the Brazilian Society of Zoology could not find a single species that had died out in a group of 300 animals, likewise when they examined their list of plants. The species-area formula would have expected a loss of about half of all species. The statement that the species are essentially "living dead"—just barely hanging on, but will eventually die out—seems almost farcical. The clearing of the Brazilian Atlantic rain forest happened in the 1800s, so we have had more than 100 years to see the "barely hanging-on species" die out, and they haven't.

In the case of Puerto Rico, where primary forest has been reduced by 99 percent over a period of 400 years, I am accused of ignoring that this loss of habitat actually resulted in the loss of seven out of sixty bird species. Yet, I clearly stated this specific fact: "*Only* seven out of sixty species of birds had become extinct" (Lomborg 2001, 254).

My main argument in *The Skeptical Environmentalist* was not that we are *not* losing biodiversity, but that we are not losing it at the rate the environmental organizations would have us believe. The criticisms presented above were not able to refute this statement—they could not provide any case-specific evidence that contradicted it. This seems like a rather poor scientific defense.

Energy

I had expected the energy chapter to be one of the chapters that was left largely unopposed. Whereas it is relatively easy to identify a problem (of course, the question is how much of a problem) in other major environmental issues, such as global warming and biodiversity, energy seems to be a clear-cut issue. The Litany that we are running out of energy has been proven wrong by history. Yet *Scientific American* (January 2002) contained an article by John P. Holdren on this specific topic. Holdren agrees that we are not running out of energy and this was precisely the main point of the chapter, so we are again faced with a critique that is concerned with more marginal issues.

Some of these issues are almost not worth mentioning. While agreeing that the coal reserves are huge, Holdren accuses me of not specifying the rate of coal use when I claim that the world has enough coal for 1,500 years. Furthermore, I wrote, air pollution control devices have removed a vast part of sulfur dioxide and nitrogen dioxide emissions in the United States. According to Holdren, I should merely have stated that the controls have caused a "moderate reduction." Aside from the insignificance of these objections, they are not very clear-cut. In the United States, sulfur dioxide pollution per quantity of coal has dropped by 75 percent since 1970. Is that only a "moderate reduction"?

Other counterarguments had more substance but were equally wrong. One of these was simply denying that concern for the depletion of resources had actually been the mainstream environmental position for decades. This line of argument is effectively contradicted by the many examples in the chapter's first section. Many influential publications at the time expressed their concern in a very direct manner: *Limits to Growth* (Meadows et al. 1972), which was translated into more than thirty languages and sold more than thirty million copies, and *The Global 2000 Report* (Barney 1980).

Holdren also claimed that although we might not be running out of energy, we are running out of environment—meaning the Earth's ecological capacity to absorb the use of energy—and we lack the ability to manage other risks of energy supply. These risks include "the political and economic dangers of overdependence on Middle East oil and the risk that nuclear systems will leak weapons materials and expertise into the hands of proliferation-prone nations or terrorists" (Holdren 2002).

This is exactly the kind of exposition that I try to counter in my book. Without using any references, Holdren manages to describe everything as growing ever worse (and even to include into the environmental agenda concepts that are far removed from its core, such as nuclear proliferation, terrorism, and economic recession from oil price hikes). Look at just one area: air pollution (estimated by the U.S. EPA to be by far the most important area). We are plainly not running out of environment or running out of the air's capacity to absorb without intolerable consequences for human well-being—all criteria pollutants in the United States have diminished in concentration over the past few decades. But Holdren simply chose a good-sounding quote ("running out of environment"), presumably in the quest to defend science, but without references and plainly incorrect.

When it is not possible to claim that we are running out of energy, the Litany seemingly urges environmentalists to point to other future problems. One is that the transition from oil to other energy sources might not be smooth and might be expensive. It is true that this could be the case (nobody can predict anything 100 percent), but my basic argument is that a crisis like that is indeed very unlikely—we have had this kind of fear, of running out, many times, and each time it has proven incorrect. Moreover, we have good reason to believe that the many different energy sources can give us sufficient energy in the future and at competitive prices.

Global Warming

Contrary to the response I anticipated to the chapter on energy, I knew that my chapter on global warming would draw attention. I hoped that this attention could spur a constructive debate. Although this has fortunately turned out to be the case in many public spheres, this has not happened in a circle of some environmental experts. In *Scientific American* (January 2002), Stephen Schneider launches an attack on my chapter on global warming. Besides criticizing my use of references, as I mentioned earlier, Schneider challenges my basic arguments:

- Temperature changes will turn out to be at the low end of the IPCC uncertainty range, which is from 1.5°C to 5.8°C if carbon dioxide were to double and be held fixed over time. Similarly, temperatures will increase much less than the maximum IPCC estimates. The temperature rise might even be lower than the lowest IPCC scenario.

- Benefits of avoiding climate change could be substantial. However, compared with the costs of trying to constrain carbon dioxide emissions, it is likely that the most economical option is to conduct business close to business-as-usual.

- The Kyoto Protocol is very expensive and will have a negligible impact on the future temperature.

Schneider sweeps aside as wishful thinking my main argument that renewable energy will crowd fossil fuel off the market in the future so effectively that the IPCC overestimates the increase in carbon dioxide. He is wrong to do so. For one thing, it is important to realize that the IPCC's scenarios are not predictions of the future but narratives—or "computer-aided storytelling" as the IPCC calls them—of possible futures. And if these stories generating the worst outcome are consistently unlikely, then there could be a real risk that we end up spending a vast amount of resources to combat threats that only occur in highly unlikely storytelling. The more likely prediction is that fossil fuels will be phased out within this century. A peer-reviewed model that I included in the book shows that if the current efficiency trend continues for renewable energy, it would mean the end of fossil fuels before the end of the century (Chakravorty, Roumasset, and Tse 1997). Thus, there is nothing to indicate that the prediction is based on wishful thinking. If Schneider was aware of any other study that has looked at the relative costs of renewables and fossil fuels over time, taking into account the remarkable increase in efficiency of renewables over the past decades, that showed that renewables will not take over, it is puzzling that these have not been presented.

Schneider also engages in a critique of the book's presentation of the cost-benefit calculations in connection with global warming. He finds it perplexing that I only cite one figure for the benefits of avoiding global warming but a whole range of estimates for trying to constrain carbon dioxide emissions. In addition, Schneider refers to studies that show that carbon dioxide emissions could actually be reduced below zero costs in order to show that the cost estimates presented might be biased upward.

It is correct that I present one cost estimate for global warming ($5 trillion), which is to be interpreted as the price we would have to pay if we do nothing about global warming. This is the figure estimated by Nordhaus and Boyer (2000) and is well in accordance with the IPCC's estimate of an annual cost of 1.5 percent to 2 percent of the global GDP toward the end of the century. It is also true that I cite a range of climate policy costs, spanning from $3 trillion to $33 trillion. However, these figures are the extra costs of choosing different emission-cut policies. Hence, they are the additional cost to the world after the cost of doing nothing has been subtracted. For instance, the Nordhaus-Boyer estimate for global stabilizing policies (a kind of global Kyoto) would be around $8.5 trillion, which is $3.5 trillion more than had we done nothing. Clearly, you cannot compare the $5 trillion with the range of $3 trillion to $33 trillion, because the $5 trillion includes the cost of global warming while the range denotes the extra cost. This also shows that why the complaint of range versus single number is entirely misplaced. You can only "do nothing" in exactly one way, whereas you can do "other things" in many ways.

Schneider's argument that some carbon dioxide emissions could be cut with net benefits is totally valid—it is also totally standard and not in any way in opposition to my arguments. The question is not whether there are below-zero-cost ways to cut some emissions, but how much can be cut at below-zero cost and the cost of more stringent cuts.

I try to point out the costs and benefits of our different policy choices, and yes, I point out that the benefit of Kyoto will be to postpone global warming in 2100 by six years yet the cost of Kyoto each year will be as great as the one-off cost of giving clean drinking water and sanitation to every single human being forever (Lomborg 2001, 315).

The book clearly showed the Kyoto Protocol will have very little effect on global warming, and it is good to see that Schneider concurs with that finding. However, he then claims that the Kyoto Protocol is a "straw-man" policy because we should be doing much more. Now, this entails both an analytic and a democratic problem. To take the democratic first: Almost all democratic discussions are about choosing or not choosing Kyoto. As this is the deal offered, would it not be reasonable to discuss the actual outcome of the deal? Likewise, if Schneider contends that the real issue is not Kyoto but something much more restrictive, would it not be democratically more honest to say that the decision is not Kyoto but something much more stringent (and hence, much more costly)?

The other analytic problem is that Schneider only talks about my analysis of Kyoto and actually neglects that I dealt with a range of much more stringent policies (which was where the $3 trillion–33 trillion range came from). This seems odd, to say the least. Of course, if Schneider wants to advocate a policy of much-more-than-Kyoto, that is fine, but the cost-benefit analyses are very clear on the issue. Almost irrespective of how it is implemented, Kyoto is a bad deal, and going even further is a much worse deal.

This was absolutely the central issue of the book, which Schneider ignores: All cost-benefit analyses show that high carbon reductions are not justified. "A central conclusion from a meeting of all economic modelers was: Current assessments determine that the 'optimal' policy calls for a relatively modest level of control of CO_2" (Lomborg 2001, 318).

In conclusion, the critics have not shown why there is a need for science to defend itself against my book. My book clearly makes a claim to be science and to be factually based. I openly state the facts and my sources, and thus anybody is free to point out where these are faulty or incorrect. None of the claims of "misrepresentation," "incomplete use of data," and "misunderstanding of the underlying science" are substantiated by the above critics. Science has no reason to defend itself against my book—whether the same is the case with alarmist environmentalism seems to be another matter.

Conclusion

The world is not going down the drain. In many areas, we are experiencing significant progress; in other areas, the pace of improvement is more moderate; and in some areas, we are without a doubt faced with problems that call for particular attention and mobilization of resources. That is why it is so necessary to measure and prioritize among the world's many problems without being blinded by the environmental Litany. In the course of this chapter, various environmental myths have been confronted with empirical facts, and the reader has been presented with the type of criticism that followed in the wake of my challenging the existing myths. I hope this has left the reader not only with an awareness that environmental doom and degradation are not just around the corner, but also with an impression of the dismay that saying this has caused in some parts of the scientific community. Equally important, the reader should have obtained a notion of the magnitude of many of the environmental problems facing the world. To make the best decisions, we need to be rational and well-considered in our use of resources and compare the benefits with the costs—this holds true not only for environmental issues but also for other major issues influencing our livelihood and the planet we inhabit.

It has to be recognized that trying to fix one problem draws resources away from fixing other problems. Hence, addressing the problem of global warming now in order to help the developing world in the future must be compared with dealing with other current, pressing issues in the developing world such as hunger, poverty, and lack of clean drinking water.

This chapter's message is a simple one: We need to do what *does* good—not just what feels good. In order to do this, we need to base our prioritizations not on fear, but on facts.

This is not always easy because the information we receive contains predominately negative news about an ever-deteriorating environment. Environmental organizations (being interest organizations) argue for their own causes, the media rely mostly on bad news to attract attention, and an important part of any researcher's job is to research a wide range of potential future problems. Therefore, to have a rational, political-decision-making process we must bear in mind that the stream of information we are receiving about the environment could very well be unbalanced. The real state of the world is that children born today will live longer, be healthier, and have access to more food. They will be better educated and benefit from more civil and political liberties. They will grow up in a world where the environment is not being destroyed, but where ecological problems in some form or another will surely continue to exist and environmental politics will still be called for. The hope is that the politics will be guided more by reason and less by the environmental Litany of doom.

Notes

1. A prime example is Al Gore comparing anyone not entirely convinced of the supremacy of the environmental question with nazism (see, for example, Gore 1992, 272).

2. Strictly speaking, this is not true because "better and better" also has ethical connotations (what is better?), but this will usually be quite uncontroversial. For example, is it better for an infant to have a better chance of survival? The difference between "is" and "ought" presented here stems originally from David Hume (1740, 468–69).

3. It should be pointed out that these small fluctuations up or down are not really decisive, given the great uncertainties and model estimates inherent in the data. Probably the best one can say about the forests is that they have neither declined nor increased significantly since 1950.

4. The rest of the Worldwatch Institute's books naturally contain many examples of these claims, but as mentioned in note 3, such singular examples are practically useless in terms of global evaluation.

5. They continue with "As noted earlier, almost half the forests that once blanketed the Earth are gone." Even setting aside the fact that this estimate is greatly exaggerated (Goudie [1993, 43] estimates 20 percent and Richards [1990, 164] 19 percent during the last three hundred years), it suggests an unreasonable comparison between a trend over a couple of decades and a trend over a couple of millennia.

6. For the last three hundred years, Goudie (1993, 43) estimates 20 percent, Williams (1994, 104) 7.5 percent, and Richards (1990, 164) 19 percent. The Intergovernmental Panel on Climate Change estimates a global forest area reduction of 20 percent from 1850 to 1990 (IPCC 2001, 3.2.2.2).

7. A problem of definition that could be applied to as much as 33 percent of the currently forested area—this is unclear from provisional descriptions, although the northern forests cover 1.2 billion ha (Stocks 1991, 197). Aldrich was not aware of other historical accounts of forest loss and was happy to receive a copy of the references in note 6.

8. In the period 1980–1995, the world lost 180 million ha (FAO 1997, 16) and for 1990–1995, 56.3 million ha (17), which is the total forested area at 3,454 million ha (10). For the 1980s (in million ha): 3,634 $(1 - 0.346$ percent$)^{10}$ = 3510.3 and for 1990–1995 (in million ha): 3510.3 $(1 - 0.32$ percent$)^5$ = 3,454. When I told Mark Aldrich at the WCMC about the claims of increasing deforestation, he said candidly, "Well, that sounds like the WWF."

9. WWF 1997c; 1998b, 36; 1999, 27, with the forest cover for 1990 being 3,410 million ha, compared with 3,454 + 56.3 = 3,510.3 million ha in 1990 (FAO 1997, 10, 17).

10. $1 - 3,410 \div 6,793 = 49.8$ percent instead of $1 - 3,044 \div 8,080 = 62.3$ percent.

11. "Only about 3 percent of the world's forests are forest plantations" (FAO 1999a, 1). Compare, however, an FAO estimate in 1997: Plantations in the industrialized world total approximately 80 to 100 Mha, in the developing world 81.2 Mha out of a total forest area of 3,454 million ha, that is, 5.2 percent (FAO 1997, 10, 14; WWF 1998a, 36).

12. Greenpeace, *Protecting Biodiversity*. Online: http://www.greenpeace.org/comms/cbio/bdfact.html. This link is now removed because of my criticism.

13. We will ignore here that the whole metaphor is biased toward stationary thinking. Although it is likely that population will increase, we will also develop ever better grains, making the minimum area smaller and smaller.

14. Of course, this also includes a distributional issue. If England has a longer and more agreeable growing season, Ethiopia may get more stifling heat—but then under the cooling scenario, when England got colder climates, Ethiopia must have benefited.

15. 4,131 deaths from excessive cold versus 2,114 deaths from excessive heat, 1987–1989 and 1994–1996 (National Safety Council 1990, 10; 1999, 16). For the United Kingdom, Subak et al. (2000, 19) find that "a warmer climate would lead to additional deaths in extreme summer heat waves but these would be more than offset by the decrease in winter mortality." See Moore (1998) for other considerations of heat benefits.

16. Each African had 2,439.4 calories/day in 1998 (FAO 2000a).

17. Although I of course would like to document the (in)efficiency of past decisions, such evaluations are rarely ever available. Apparently, making a cost-benefit analysis of a decision already made and effectuated would be somewhat pointless as it could make no difference.

18. This myth is invoked by, for example, the Worldwatch Institute: "Just as a continuously growing cancer eventually destroys its life-support systems by destroying its host, a continuously expanding global economy is slowly destroying its host—the Earth's ecosystem" (Worldwatch Institute, 1998a, 4; compare Worldwatch Institute 2001, 12). It stems originally from the 1973 Ehrlich claim of negative environmental impact being determined multiplicatively by population size, affluence, and technology (sometimes written I = PAT; see Common 1996). Consequently, this relationship by definition makes affluence affect the environment negatively (although its impact can be temporarily tempered by technological progress).

19. Conspicuously, this tradeoff is central to the new IPCC scenarios, where a choice between the economy and the environment is one of the two main dimensions. See IPCC (2000, 28).

20. Not all research, of course. However, basic research generally does not generate any public awareness, and if it should do so, there is no reason to suppose that it will systematically do so in a positive way, negating the following mechanism of negative lopsidedness.

21. *Ingeniøren* (*The engineer*), 26 (1996): 14.

22. *Ingeniøren* (*The engineer*), 28 (1996): 8.

23. Named the second and the twenty-first most powerful lobbies in Washington by *Fortune* (Birnbaum and Graves 1999). See also critical discussion of the AFBF as lobbyists in Rauber and McManus (1994).

24. Polls show that people have much more trust in the environmental groups to protect the environment than they have in business (78 percent versus 38 percent) or even in the EPA (72 percent) (Dunlap 2000).

References

Abrahamsen, Gunnar, Arne O. Stuames, and Bjørn Tveite, eds. 1994. *Long-term experiments with acid rain in Norwegian forest ecosystems*. New York: Springer-Verlag.

Asimov, Isaac, and Frederik Pohl. 1991. *Our angry earth*. New York: Tom Doherty Associates.

Birnbaum, Jeffrey H., and Natasha Graves. 1999. How to buy clout in the capital. *Fortune* 140 (11): 207–8.

Boehmer-Christiansen, Sonja. 1997. A winning coalition of advocacy: Climate research, bureaucracy and "alternative" fuels. *Energy Policy* 25 (4): 439–44.

Bongaarts, John. 2002. Population: Ignoring its impact. *Scientific American* (January).

Brander, James A., and M. Scott Taylor. 1998. The simple economics of Easter Island: A Ricardo-Malthus model of renewable resource use. *American Economic Review* 88 (1): 119–38.

Brown, Lester. 1996. Who will feed China? *Futurist* 30 (1): 14–18.

Chakravorty, Ujjayant, James Roumasset, and Kinping Tse. 1997. Endogeneous substitution among energy resources and global warming. *Journal of Political Economy* 105 (6): 1, 201–34.

Common, Michael. 1996. Consumption and the environment. Background paper, Department of the Environment, Sport and Territories, Commonwealth of Australia. Online: http://www.environment.gov.au/epcg/eeu/consumption/bgpaper.htm.

Danish Environmental Assessment Institute. 2002. Assessing the ecological footprint—a look at the WWF living planet report 2002 (September). Online: http://www.imv.dk/include/downloadfile.asp?file_id={440A67A22DD7692D45D82D84ED2D0FF60D04EFF3}.

Dunlap, Riley E. 2000. Americans have positive image of the environmental movement: Majorities agree with movement's goals, and trust it to protect the nation's environment. *Gallup Poll Releases*, April 18. Online: http://www.gallup.com/poll/releases/pr000418.asp.

European Environment Agency. 2000. Data service. Online: http://warehouse.eea.eu.int.

Ehrlich, Paul R. 1970. Looking back from 2000 A.D. *The Progressive* (April): 23–25.

Ehrlich, Paul R., and Anne H. Ehrlich. 1974. *The end of affluence: A blueprint for your future.* New York: Ballantine Books.

Energy Information Administration. 2002. International Energy Outlook 2002. Washington, D.C.: Energy Information Administration under U.S. Department of Energy. Online: http://www.eia.doe.gov/oiaf/ieo/index.html.

Fairhead, James, and Melissa Leach. 1998. *Reframing deforestation: Global analysis and local realities: Studies in West Africa.* London: Routledge.

Falkenmark, Malin, and Jan Lundqvist. 1997. World freshwater problems: Call for a new realism. Background document for CSD 1997. Stockholm: Stockholm Environment Institute.

Food and Agriculture Organization of the United Nations (FAO). 1996. World Food Summit: Technical Background Documents, I-XV. Online: http://www.fao.org/wfs/.

FAO. 1997. State of the world's forests 1997. Rome. Online: http://www.fao.org/montes/fo/sofo/SOFO97/97toc-e.stm.

———. 1999a. State of the world's forests 1999. Rome. Online: http://www.fao.org/forestry/FO/SOFO/SOFO99/sofo99-e.stm.

———. 1999b. The state of food insecurity in the world 1999. Rome. Online: http://www.fao.org/FOCUS/E/SOFI/home-e.htm.

———. 2000a. Database. Rome. Online: http://apps.fao.org/.

———. 2000b. *Agriculture: Toward 2015/30.* Technical Interim Report, April. Rome. Online: http://www.fao.org/es/esd/at2015/toc-e.htm.

Gonick, Larry, and Alice Outwater. 1996. *The cartoon guide to the environment.* New York: HarperPerennial.

Gore, Al. 1992. *Earth in the balance: Ecology and the human spirit.* Boston: Houghton Mifflin.

Goudie, Andrew. 1993. *The human impact on the natural environment.* Oxford: Blackwell.

Greenpeace. 1992. *The environmental legacy of the Gulf War.* A Greenpeace Report. Online: http://www.greenpeace.org/gopher/campaigns/military/1992/gulfwar3.txt.

Gwynne, Peter. 1975. The cooling world. *Newsweek,* April 28, 64.

Holdren, John P. 2002. Energy: Asking the wrong question. *Scientific American* (January).

Hume, David. 1739, 1740. *A treatise of human nature,* ed. L. A. Selby-Bigge and P. H. Nidditch. Oxford: Oxford University Press.

Hume, David. 1777. Of the populousness of ancient nations. In *Essays: Moral, Political and Literary,* Part II, Essay XI. Indianapolis, Ind.: Liberty Fund, 377–464.

Intergovernmental Panel on Climate Change (IPCC). 2000. Special report on emission scenarios, special report of Working Group III of the IPCC. Online: http://www.grida.no/climate/ipcc/emission/index.htm; summary at http://www.ipcc.ch/pub/SPM_SRES.pdf.

———. 2001. *Climate change 2001: The scientific basis,* ed. J. T. Houghton, Y. Ding, D. J. Griggs, M. Noguer, P. J. van der Linden, and D. Xiaosu. Contribution of Working Group I to the Third Assessment Report of the IPCC. Cambridge: Cambridge University Press.

Knudsen, Jørgen. 1997. *Den store fortælling om synd og straf* (The great story of sin and punishment). In *Livet i drivhuset—en debatbog om miljø og samfund* (Life in the greenhouse—a debate book on the environment and the Society), by Peder Agger, Lennart Emborg, and Jørgen S. Nørgård. Copenhagen: Mellemfolkeligt Samvirke, 36–47.

Leach, Melissa, and James Fairhead. 1999. Challenging environmental orthodoxies: The case of West African deforestation. *Renewable Energy for Development* 11 (1): 1, 8–10.

Lomborg, Bjørn. 2001. *The skeptical environmentalist.* New York: Cambridge University Press.

Lovejoy, Thomas E. 1980. A projection of species extinctions. In The global 2000 report to the president of the U.S.: Entering the 21st Century I–III, ed. Gerald O. Barney. New York: Pergamon Press, 328–31.

———. 2002. Biodiversity: Dismissing scientific process. *Scientific American* (January).

Mann, Charles C. 1991. Extinction: Are ecologists crying wolf? *Science* 253: 736–38.

Meadows, Donella H., Dennis L. Meadows, Jørgen Randers, and William W. Behrens III. 1972. *Limits to growth.* London: Potomac Associates Book.

Meilby, Mogens. 1996. *Journalistikkens grundtrin: Fra idé til artikel.* Aarhus: Forlaget Ajour.

Moore, Thomas Gale. 1998. Health and amenity effects of global warming. *Economic Inquiry* 36 (3): 471–98.

Myers, Norman. 1979. *The sinking ark: A new look at the problem of disappearing species.* Oxford: Pergamon Press.

National Safety Council. 1990. Accident facts, 1990 edition. Chicago: National Safety Council.

———. 1999: Injury Facts, 1999 edition. Chicago: National Safety Council.

Nordhaus, William, and Joseph Boyer. 2000. *Warming the world: Economic models of global warming.* Cambridge, Mass.: MIT Press. Online: http://www.econ.yale.edu/%7Enordhaus/homepage/web%20table%20of%20contents%20102599.htm.

Pimm, Stuart, and Jeff Harvey. 2001. No need to worry about the future: Environmentally, we are told, "Things are getting better." *Nature* 414 (November 8): 149–50.

Poulsen, Jørgen. 1998. *Dissidentens stemme* (The voice of the dissident). *Politiken,* March 13, s2, 3–4.

Rauber, Paul, and Reed McManus. 1994. Down on the farm bureau. *Sierra* 79 (6): 32–33.

Richards, John F. 1990. Land transformation. In *The earth as transformed by human action*, by B. L. Turner II, William C. Clark, Robert W. Kates, John F. Richards, Jessica T. Mathews, and William B. Meyer. Cambridge: Cambridge University Press, 163–80.

Schneider, Stephen. 2002. Global warming: Neglecting the complexities. *Scientific American* (January): 62–65.

Simon, Julian. 1995. Why do we hear prophecies of doom from every side? *Futurist* 29 (1): 19–24.

———. 1996. *The ultimate resource 2*. Princeton, N.J.: Princeton University Press.

Stocks, Brian J. 1991. The extent and impact of forest fires in northern circumpolar countries. In *Global biomass burning: Atmospheric, climatic, and biospheric implications*, ed. Joel S. Levine. Cambridge, Mass.: MIT Press, 197–202.

Subak, S., J. P. Palutikof, M. D. Agnew, S. J. Watson, C. G. Bentham, M. G. R. Cannell, M. Hulme, S. McNally, J. E. Thornes, D. Waughray, and J. C. Woods. 2000. The impact of the anomalous weather of 1995 on the U.K. economy. *Climatic Change* 44: 1–26.

UNICEF. 2000. The state of the world's children. New York: UNICEF. Online: www.unicef.org/sowc02summary/index.html.

U.S. Bureau of the Census. 2000. *International Data Base*. Washington, D.C. Online: http://www.census.gov/ipc/www/idbnew.html.

Williams, Michael. 1994. Forests and tree cover. In *Changes in land use and land cover: A global perspective*, ed. William B. Meyer and B. L. Turner II. 1994. Cambridge: Cambridge University Press, 97–124.

Worldwatch Institute. 1998a. *State of the world 1998*, by Lester R. Brown, Christopher Flavin, Hilary F. French, and Janet Abramovitz, Chris Bright, Seth Dunn, Gary Gardner, Anne McGinn, Jennifer Mitchell, Michael Renner, David Roodman, John Tuxill, and Linda Starke, editor. New York: W. W. Norton.

———. 1998b. *Vital Signs 1998*, by Lester R. Brown, Michael Renner, Christopher Flavin, with Janet N. Abramovitz, Seth Dunn, Hilary F. French, Gary Gardner, Brian Halweil, Nicholas Lenssen, Ashley T. Mattoon, Anne Platt McGinn, Jennifer D. Mitchell, Molly O'Meara, David M. Roodman, Payal Sampat, Michael Strauss, John Tuxill, and Linda Starke, editor. New York: W. W. Norton.

———. 1999a. *State of the World 1999*, by Lester R. Brown, Christopher Flavin, Hilary French, and Janet Abramovitz, Seth Dunn, Gary Gardner, Ashley Mattoon, Anne Platt McGinn, Molly O'Meara, Michael Renner,

David Roodman, Payal Sampat, John Tuxill, and Linda Starke, editor. New York: W. W. Norton.

———. 1999b. *Vital Signs 1999*, by Lester R. Brown, Michael Renner, and Brian Halweil. New York: W. W. Norton.

———. 2000. *State of the World 2000*, by Lester R. Brown, Christopher Flavin, Hilary French, and Janet Abramovitz, Seth Dunn, Gary Gardner, Ashley Mattoon, Anne Platt McGinn, Molly O'Meara, Michael Renner, Chris Bright, Sandra Postel, Brian Halweil, and Linda Starke, editor. New York: W. W. Norton.

———. 2001. *State of the World 2001*, by Lester R. Brown, Christopher Flavin, Hilary French, Janet Abramovitz, Seth Dunn, Gary Gardner, Lisa Mastny, Ashley Mattoon, David Roodman, Payal Sampat, Molly O. Sheehan, and Linda Starke, editor. New York: W. W. Norton.

World Bank. 2000a. The 2000 world development indicators CD-ROM. Some data available at http://sima-ext.worldbank.org/data-query.

———. 2000b. Global development finance 2000. Volume I, Analysis and summary tables; Volume II, Country tables. Washington, D.C.: World Bank. Online: http://www.worldbank.org/prospects/gdf2000/.

WWF. 1997a. Global annual forest report 1997. Online: http://www.panda .org/resources/publications/forest/report97/index.htm.

———. 1997b. The year the world caught fire, by Nigel Dudley. Discussion paper, WWF International (December).

———. 1997c. 1997: The year the world caught fire. Press release (December 16). Online: http://www.panda.org/forests4life/news/161297_year fire.cfm.

———. 1997d. Two-thirds of the world's forests lost forever. Online: http:// www.panda.org/forests4life/news/081097_lostfor.cfm.

———. 1998a. Living planet report 1998: Overconsumption is driving the rapid decline of the world's natural environments. Gland: WWF International. Online: http://www.panda.org/livingplanet/lpr/index.htm.

———. 1998b. The year the world caught fire. Featured story. Online: http:/ /www.panda.org/news/features/01-98/story3.htm.

———. 1999. Living planet report 1999. Gland: WWF International. Online: http://www.panda.org/livingplanet/lpr99/.

———. 2002. Living planet report 2002. Gland: WWF International. Online: http://www.panda.org/livingplanet/lpr02/.

Chapter 2

Economic Growth, Technological Change, and Human Well-Being

Indur M. Goklany

IF PRESENT TRENDS continue, the world in 2000 will be more crowded, more polluted, less stable ecologically, and more vulnerable to disruption than the world we live in now. Serious stresses involving population, resources, and environment are clearly visible ahead. Despite greater material output, the world's people will be poorer in many ways than they are today.

The Global 2000 Report to the President of the U.S.: Entering the 21st Century (Barney 1980)

This neo-Malthusian vision of the future stands in sharp contrast to the conclusions in *The State of Humanity* edited by Julian Simon (1995). That monumental collection of fifty-eight chapters by more than fifty scholars documents the tremendous strides that have been made in human well-being over the centuries, as well as trends in natural

Indur M. Goklany was PERC's 2000 Julian Simon Fellow. He holds a Ph.D. in electrical engineering and has more than twenty-five years' experience addressing science and policy aspects of environmental and natural resource policy issues in state and federal government and in the private sector. He was formerly chief of the technical assessment division of the National Commission on Air Quality and a consultant in the Office of Policy, Planning, and Evaluation at the U.S. EPA. The opinions expressed in this chapter are solely those of the author. Much of this chapter is based on Goklany (2001a).

resource use and environmental quality. Based on these discussions, Simon wrote: "Our species is better off in just about every measurable material way" (1).

Bjørn Lomborg, determined to prove Julian Simon wrong and to verify the doomsday-visions of the kind that permeated *The Global 2000 Report*, enlisted ten of his "sharpest students" to comb through the empirical data (Lomborg 2001, xix) on long-term temporal trends in human and environmental well-being. Much to his surprise, they found that although the population continues to grow, albeit at a decelerating pace, the state of humanity has never been better, that the average person on the globe has never been less hungry, better educated, richer, healthier, and longer-lived than today.[1] No less important, not only is human well-being advancing but, in many cases, so seems to be the state of the environment, especially in the rich countries of the world.

Lomborg focused mainly on temporal trends in a variety of indicators rather than on how those indicators might vary with wealth or per-capita income across countries and regions. He also looked at temporal trends in infant mortality and life expectancy for various income groups (2001, 52, 55) and, as Yandle documents in Chapter 3 of this volume, these data suggest that richer groups are better off.

In this chapter, I examine trends in several of the most critical indicators of human well-being, paying special attention to how they vary across countries as a function of economic development and technological change. In that respect, the analysis presented here complements and extends Lomborg's analysis.

This chapter examines seven indicators of human well-being.

- *Available food supplies per capita*. Having sufficient food is the first step to a healthy society. It enables the average person to live a productive life, whereas hunger and undernourishment retard education and the development of human capital, slowing down technological change and economic growth.

- *Life expectancy*. To most people, this is the single most valuable indicator of human well-being. Longer life expectancy is generally accompanied by an increase in disability-free years.

- *Infant mortality.* Throughout history, high levels of death in early childhood have produced enormous sorrow, reduced population growth, and lengthened the time women spend in childbearing.

- *Economic development.* Gross domestic product (GDP) per capita is a measure of people's income. Thus, it measures the wealth or the level of economic development of a country. Although wealth is not an end in itself, a nation's per-capita GDP indicates how well its people can achieve the ends they desire, from greater availability of food, safe water, and sanitation to higher levels of education and health care.

- *Education.* Education can be an end in itself, but it also adds to human capital and can accelerate the creation and diffusion of technology. Education (particularly of women) helps to spread knowledge of nutrition and public health practices.

- *Political rights and economic freedom.* The ability to conduct one's life creatively and productively usually depends on having political rights and economic freedom. They are critical to maintaining liberty and prosperity.

- *A composite human development index.* Using an approach similar to that employed in the United Nations Development Programme (UNDP), this index combines indicators for life expectancy, education, and per-capita income (UNDP 2000).[2]

As part of this examination, I will also address how factors contributing to or related to the improvements in these indicators vary with economic development, for example, access to safe water and sanitation, crop yields, and child labor. Have differences in human well-being widened between developed and developing countries? Do urban residents fare worse than rural residents? Finally, I discuss the factors that appear to be responsible for the remarkable cycle of progress that has accompanied modern economic growth and the improvements in human well-being over the past two centuries.

Hunger and Undernourishment

Concerns about the world's ability to feed its burgeoning population have been around at least since Thomas Malthus's "Essay on the Principle of Population" two hundred years ago. Several neo-Malthusians of the twentieth century confidently predicted apocalyptic famines in the developing countries in the latter part of the century (Ehrlich 1968; Paddock and Paddock 1967). Even though the world's population is the largest it has ever been, the average person has never been better fed.

Since 1950, the global population has increased by 90 percent, increasing the demand for food, but at the same time the real price of food commodities has declined 75 percent (Mitchell and Ingco 1993; World Resources Institute 1998). Greater agricultural productivity and international trade have made this possible (Goklany 1998). As a result, average daily food supplies per person increased 24 percent globally from 1961 to 1998, as indicated by Table 2.1, and the increase for developing countries was even larger at 38 percent.

The Food and Agriculture Organization (FAO) estimates the minimum daily energy requirement for maintaining health and body weight and engaging in light physical activity to be between 1,720 and 1,960 calories (properly, kilocalories) per person per day (1996a). Adding an allowance for moderate activity to this threshold results in an estimate of the national average requirement of 2,000 to 2,310 calories per person per day. (This assumes equal food provisions are likely to be equally available to the population.)

Especially remarkable are the improvements in India and China since the middle of the twentieth century. By 1998, China's food supplies had gone up 82 percent from a barely subsistence level of 1,636 calories per person per day in 1961. India's food supplies went up 51 percent, from 1,635 calories per person per day compared with the

Table 2.1
Daily Food Supplies, c. 1790–1998
(kilocalories per capita per day)

Area	Pre- or Early Industrial Phase	1961	1975	1985	1998
France	1,753 (1790)	3,193	3,246	3,498	3,541
Developed Countries		2,948	3,144	3,284	3,246
India	1,635 (1950–1951)	2,073	1,942	2,143	2,466
China	2,115 (1947–1948)	1,636	2,084	2,616	2,972
Developing Countries		1,930	2,146	2,421	2,663
Sub-Saharan Africa		2,056	2,090	2,043	2,221
World		2,255	2,423	2,637	2,792

Note: Pre- or early industrial phase data are for the year(s) shown in parentheses; data for China are based on 22 provinces. Many developing countries, such as India and China, barely embarked on industrialization until after World War II.

Sources: Burnette and Mokyr (1995); FAO (2000); Fogel (1995); Goklany (1999a)

1950–1951 average. Increases in food supplies reduced the number of chronically undernourished people in developing countries from an average of 920 million in 1969–1971 to less than 800 million (on average) from 1995–1997 (or from 35 percent to 19 percent of their population) despite a 70 percent growth in population (FAO 1996b, 1999).

Figure 2.1, based on cross-country data for 1961 and 1994 from the World Resources Institute (1998), shows that available food supplies per capita per day increase with GDP per capita as well as with time. To better illustrate the change in food supplies for low-income people, the scale on the graph ends at a GDP per capita of $10,000 (in 1995 dollars).[3] The upward slope for each year probably reflects the fact that the wealthier the country, the greater its ability to afford more productive technologies to increase crop yields or purchase food in the global market. The upward shift of the available food supply curve between 1961 and 1994 resulted from technological improvement. This technological change allowed food production to outpace population

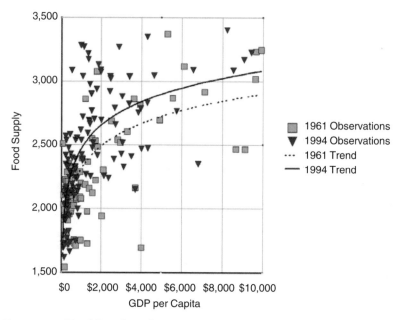

Figure 2.1   Food Supply and Income, 1961–1964

Note: Food supply data in kilocalories per day, per capita; income is expressed as GDP per capita in 1995 US$ at market exchange rates (MXR).

Source: World Resources Institute (1998)

growth (Goklany 1998). As a result, the real global price of food commodities declined 75 percent since 1950 (Mitchell and Ingco 1993; World Resources Institute 1998), and for any given level of income, more food was available in 1994 than in 1961.

Life Expectancy

Life expectancy at birth is probably the single most important indicator of human well-being. For much of human history, life expectancy was 20 to 30 years (Preston 1995). As Table 2.2 indicates, by 1998 it had increased to 66.9 years worldwide (UNDP 2000), and for developed countries, life expectancy at birth was 74.5 years in 1998.

Table 2.2
Life Expectancy at Birth, in Years, Middle Ages to 1998

Area	Middle Ages	Pre- or Early Industrial Phase	1950–1955	1975–1980	1998
France		−30 (1800)	66.5	73.7	78.2
United Kingdom	20–30	35.9 (1799–1803)	69.2	72.8	77.3
Developed Countries	20–30		66.5	72.2	74.5
India		24–25 (1901–1911)	38.7	52.9	62.9
China		25–35 (1929–1931)	40.8	65.3	70.1
Africa			37.8	47.9	53.8
Developing Countries			40.9	56.7	63.6
World	20–30		46.5	59.7	66.9

Note: Pre- or early industrial phase data are for the year(s) shown in parentheses; U.K. data for 1799–1803 are for England and Wales only; data for Africa and Developing Countries for 1998 are for 1995–2000 from the World Resource Institute (1998).

Sources: Lee and Feng (1999); Preston (1995); Wrigley and Schofield (1981, 529); World Resources Institute (1998); UNDP (2000)

Not only does life expectancy increase over time, it increases with per-capita income. Comparing data for 1962 and 1997, Figure 2.2 shows that a country with a GDP per capita of $300 per year would have increased its citizens' average life expectancy from 44.7 years in 1962 to 55.0 in 1997.[4]

Figure 2.2 also suggests that developing countries may have higher life expectancies than did the developed countries at equivalent levels of income. This, indeed, is the case for China and India, countries once synonymous with poverty and wretchedness. In 1913, when the United States had a GDP per capita of $5,305 (in 1990 dollars), life expectancy at birth was 52 years[5] (Bureau of the Census 1975). In 1995, when China and India had GDP per capita of a mere $2,653 and $1,568 respectively (also in 1990 dollars), they had life expectancies of approximately 69 and 62 years (World Bank 1999).

By and large, life expectancies continue to climb worldwide. However, life expectancies have dropped since the late 1980s and early

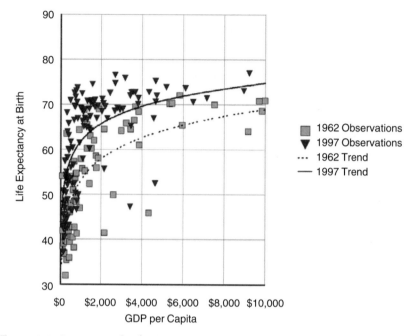

Figure 2.2   Income and Life Expectancy at Birth, 1962–1997

Note: Data represent the life expectancy at birth in years; income is expressed as GDP per capita in 1995 US$ at MXR.

Source: World Bank (1999)

1990s in many countries where economies have deteriorated. Russia's life expectancy, for example, declined 3.9 years between 1989 and 2000 (World Bank 2002). Over this period, its GDP per capita (in real dollars) declined 35 percent (World Bank 2002). Yields of cereal, which represent 50 percent of all crops, fell (Goklany 1998), and food supplies per capita, nutritional levels, and public health services all declined. Alcoholism increased, as did accidental deaths, homicides, hypertension, and suicides (Becker and Bloom 1998). Life expectancies have similarly declined in other Eastern European and former Soviet Union countries (EEFSU). Life expectancies also are declining in a number of sub-Saharan countries, seemingly due to a vicious cycle involving

Table 2.3
Infant Mortality, Middle Ages to 1998

Area	Middle Ages	Pre- or Early Industrial Phase	1950– 1955	1975– 1980	1998
Sweden		240 (1800)	22	8	4
France		182 (1830)	45	11	5
Developed Countries	>200		58	18	9
China			195	52	38
India			190	129	69
Developing Countries			179	98	64
Africa			185	120	91
World	>200		156	87	58

Note: Data represent the number of deaths before age one per 1,000 live births. Pre- or early industrial phase data are for the years shown in parentheses.

Sources: Hill (1995); Mitchell (1992, 116-23); UNDP (2000); World Resources Institute (1998)

HIV/AIDS, malaria, and a drop in economic output (UNDP 2000, Goklany 2002a).

Infant Mortality

Before industrialization, at least one out of every five children died before reaching his or her first birthday (see Table 2.3), but the rate fell to 58 per 1,000 live births worldwide in 1998. This is the same level that more developed countries had reached in the 1950 to 1955 period (World Resources Institute 1998; UNDP 2000). As recently as 1900, infant mortality in the United States was about 160; in 1997, it was about seven (Bureau of the Census 1975, 60; 1999).

In developing countries, the declines started later, but may be occurring more rapidly in some areas. For instance, between the early 1950s and 1998, India's infant mortality fell from 190 to 69, and China's from 195 to 38 (World Resources Institute 1998; UNDP 2000).

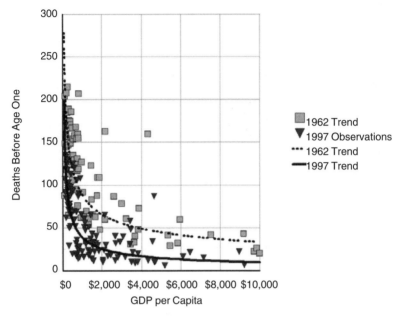

Figure 2.3   Infant Mortality and Income, 1962–1997
Note: Infant mortality is the number of deaths before age one per 1,000 live births; income is expressed as GDP per capita in 1995 US$ at MXR.
Source: World Bank (1999)

It is well known that infant mortality declines as a nation's income increases (see, for example, Pritchett and Summers 1996; World Bank 1993). Figure 2.3 illustrates this relationship (using data for 1962 and 1997). It also shows the general worldwide decline in infant mortality over time that is a consequence of technological change. It dropped from a global average of 114 in 1962 to 56 in 1997 (World Bank 1999).[6]

Economic Development

Long-term trends in economic growth, based on data from Maddison (1998, 1999), are shown in Table 2.4 for the United States, India, China, Africa, Europe, and the world. While these estimates are less

Table 2.4
Gross Domestic Product per Capita, A.D. 1–1995

Area	1	1000	1500	1700	1820	1952	1995
Europe	~$425	$400	~$640	$870	$1,129	$4,374	$13,951
United States	400	400	400	600	1,260	10,645	23,377
India				531	531	609	1,568
China	450	450	600	600	600	537	3,196
Africa	400	400	400	400	400		1,221
World	425	420	545	604	673	2,268	5,194

Note: In 1990 international dollars (see endnote 9). Data for Europe A.D. 1 and 1500 are based on Maddison (1999), using arithmetical average for "Western Europe" and the "Rest of Europe." Data for USA A.D. 1 to 1500 are based on Maddison's (1999) estimate for "North America." Data for Africa are assumed to be a straight line until 1820.
Sources: Maddison (1998, 1999)

than precise, they do indicate that for most of the last two millennia, GDP per capita worldwide was below $600, measured in 1990 international dollars.[7] Today it is more than eight times that.

In addition to incomes being higher, basic necessities such as food are cheaper than they were even a few decades ago. For instance, between the years 1897 to 1902 and 1992 to 1994, U.S. retail prices of flour, bacon, and potatoes relative to per-capita income dropped by 92 percent, 87 percent, and 80 percent, respectively (Goklany 1999c).

Not only is food cheaper and the average person's annual income higher, but workers spend fewer hours on the job. Between 1870 and 1992, average hours worked per person employed declined 46 percent, 48 percent, and 36 percent for the United States, France, and Japan, respectively. Ausubel and Grübler (1995) estimate that for the average British worker, total life hours worked declined from 124,000 in 1856 to 69,000 in 1981. Because the average Briton lives longer and works fewer hours each year, the life hours worked by the average British worker have declined from 50 percent to 20 percent of his or her "disposable" life hours.[8] In other words, the average person has more disposable time for leisure, hobbies, and personal development. Nota-

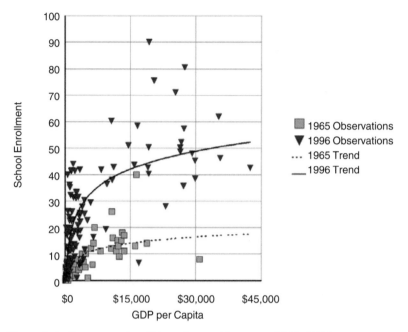

Figure 2.4   Postsecondary Education and Income, 1965–1996
Note: School enrollment expressed as the percent of relevant population; GDP per capita is in 1995 US$ at MXR.
Source: World Bank (1999)

bly, the above calculation did not account for the advent of cheap and better lighting which, if nothing else, has increased the menu of activities that individuals might choose to undertake in nondaylight hours.

Education

Figure 2.4 shows that the percent of the eligible population enrolled in postsecondary education increased with time and with affluence across a range of countries (World Bank 1999).[9] Table 2.5 shows long-term improvements in the levels of education for the United States, France, Japan, China, and India based on data from Maddison (1995, 1998).

Literacy has increased worldwide as well. Between 1970 and 1997,

Table 2.5
Education, Average Number of Years per Person, c. 1820–1992

Area	1820	1870	1913	1950	1973	1992
France			6.99	9.58	11.69	15.96
United States	1.75	3.92	7.86	11.27	14.58	18.04
Japan	1.50	1.50	5.36	9.11	12.09	14.87
India				1.35	2.60	5.55
China				1.60	4.09	8.93

Note: Data represent the average number of years per person aged 16-64.
Sources: Maddison (1995, 1998)

global illiteracy rates dropped from 45.8 percent to 25.6 percent. Complementing these increases are declines in the portion of the population aged ten to fourteen years who are working. Worldwide child labor measured this way has declined from 24.0 percent in 1960 to 12.6 percent in 1997 (World Bank 1999).

Political and Economic Freedom

Economic freedom is also ascendant around the world. Gwartney and his coworkers have constructed an index of economic freedom that takes into consideration personal choice, protection of private property, and freedom to use, exchange, or give property to another. According to this index, economic freedom increased in the 1990s in ninety-eight of the 116 countries for which they had data. Their analysis indicates that the more economically free a country's population, the higher its economic growth (Gwartney, Holcombe, and Lawson 1998; Gwartney, Lawson, and Samida 2000). See Figure 2.5.

Human Development Index

Each of the above indicators makes a strong case for a steady increase in many aspects of human well-being, but it is also possible to create a

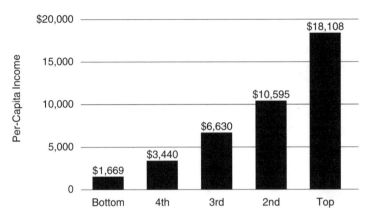

Figure 2.5   Economic Freedom Rankings by Quintiles for 116 Countries
Source: Gwartney, Lawson, and Samida (2000)

single index that incorporates a number of key measurements of well-being. The United Nations Development Program (UNDP) has popularized this approach with its Human Development Index (HDI). This index is based on life expectancy, education, and GDP per capita.[10]

According to the UNDP's *Human Development Report* (2001), the HDI has been going up for most countries. This index is somewhat arbitrary and probably understates improvements because it omits measurements of hunger and infant mortality. Nevertheless, as Figure 2.6 shows, since 1975—the first year for which that report provides data—the population-weighted HDI has improved for the so-called high, middle, and low development tiers of countries, as well as for sub-Saharan Africa (two-thirds of which are also included in the low development tier). The data indicate that human well-being has improved and continues to improve for the vast majority of the world's population. Over the past decade or so, however, well-being has been reduced in some sub-Saharan and EEFSU countries.

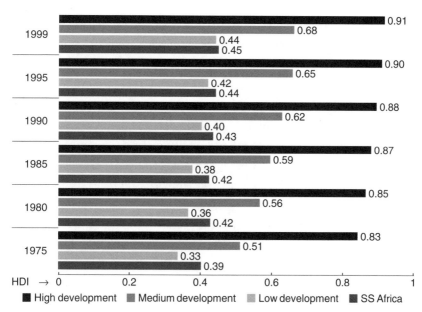

Figure 2.6   Human Development Index, 1975–1999
Note: The HDI scale tops out at 1 unit.
Sources: UNDP (2001), World Bank (2001)

Have Gaps in Human Well-Being Widened?

There can be no doubt that human well-being has improved continually over the past two centuries, but some people and organizations still claim that inequalities between the developed and developing nations continue to widen. Here is a typical observation, this one from the UNDP's *Human Development Report 1999*:

> Nearly 30 years ago the Pearson Commission began its report with the recognition that "the widening gap between the developed and developing countries has become the central problem of our times." But over the past three decades the income gap between the richest fifth and the poorest fifth has more than doubled. . . . Narrowing the gaps between rich and poor . . . should become explicit global goals. . . . (11)

Indeed, as Table 2.4 shows, there are wide—and, in many cases, growing—disparities in income between the richer and the poorer countries. The gaps in per-capita income between Western Europe and the United States and other regions have ballooned since 1700 (Maddison 1998, 1999), and many people remain terribly poor. According to the UNDP (2000), 1.2 billion people, mainly in the developing world, live in "absolute poverty" (defined as subsisting on less than US$1 per day), and at least thirty-five nations had lower per-capita incomes in 1998 than in 1975 (measured in real dollars). These claims have become a rallying cry for the forces that oppose globalization (see, for example, Goklany 2002a).

However, a number of recent studies have disputed the claim that income inequalities have been widening in recent decades. Dollar and Kraay, pro-globalization economists at the World Bank, have challenged such statements, countering that "the best evidence available shows the exact opposite to be true . . . [and that] . . . the current wave of globalization, which started around 1980, has actually promoted economic equality and reduced poverty" (2000b).

More recently, development economist Xavier Sala-i-Martin found that poverty rates declined substantially between the 1970s and 1998 (2002). Worldwide between 1976 and 1998, despite a population increase of 43 percent (FAO 2003), the number of people subsisting on an income of $1 a day declined from 16.1 percent to 6.7 percent of the population, or by 235 million, while those living on an income of $2 a day declined from 39.1 percent to 18.6 percent, or by 450 million (Sala-i-Martin 2002, 36). The bulk of the decline took place in Asia. Latin America reduced poverty overall, but most of the reduction occurred during the 1970s with little or no reduction after that. On the other hand, the number of people living in poverty in Africa increased by 175 million people (from 22 percent to 44 percent of the population) according to the one-dollar definition and by 227 million (from 53 to 64 percent) according to the two-dollar definition.

However, if consumption, rather than income, is used to determine the $1- and $2-a-day poverty levels, then for any given year the portion of the population (as well as the numbers) living in poverty goes up. For instance, in 1998 the $1-a-day poverty rate based on income was 6.7 percent compared with 16.0 percent had it been based on consumption (Sala-i-Martin 2002, 36). The latter figure works out closer to the now-familiar 1.2 billion people estimated to live in absolute poverty (or on less than $1 a day). Notably, consumption-based global poverty levels also declined between 1976 and 1998—from 31.0 percent to 16.0 percent using the dollar-a-day definition and from 53.1 percent to 34.7 percent using the two-dollar definition (Sala-i-Martin 2002, 36).

Sala-i-Martin, using each of nine separate indices of income inequality, also showed substantial reductions in global income inequality during the 1980s and 1990s. Thus, it seems that claims of increasing poverty and rising income inequality in the recent past are not substantiated by data.

More important, what about gaps in other, more significant indicators of human well-being, such as hunger, infant mortality, life expectancy, education, and child labor? After all, as we have already seen, the importance of economic development stems from its ability to help improve these measures of welfare. The central issue is not whether income gaps are growing, but whether wealth and globalization advance well-being, and if inequalities in well-being have indeed expanded, whether that is because the rich have advanced at the expense of the poor.

Consider the trends in life expectancy, perhaps the single most important indicator of human well-being. Before industrialization, life expectancy at birth was about thirty years. But because the rich countries discovered, developed, and adopted modern public health and medical technologies first, large gaps in life expectancy had opened up between rich and poor countries by the mid-1900s. But these gaps have since shrunk because of the diffusion of those technologies owing to trade in and transfer of ideas, goods, and services from rich to poor. From 1960 to 1990, relative to high-income in the Organisation for

Economic Co-operation and Development countries (HiOECD), the gap for medium-income countries declined from 24.5 to 8.1 years; that for low-income countries declined from 25.7 to 18.8 years; and that for sub-Saharan Africa dropped from 29.4 to 26.4. Cross-country analysis for any specific year also indicates that, generally, richer is also longer-lived. It seems counterintuitive, however, that the lower the initial gap, the faster it closed (because the higher the life expectancy, the harder should it have been to raise further). But that is consistent with the fact that groups that lagged in globalization also lagged economically and in access to health technologies and should, therefore, have found it harder to close the life expectancy gap (Goklany 2002a).

Similar patterns were exhibited by trends related to other critical measures of well-being—such as freedom from hunger, infant mortality, and child labor between the 1960s and the late 1990s—and, between 1975 and 1999, for trends related to the UNDP's human development index. In each case, the indicators generally improved with wealth and the passage of time, and gaps in the indicators (relative to HiOECD) shrank the least for sub-Saharan Africa and the most for medium-income countries (Goklany 2002a).

From 1990 to 1999, however, life expectancy gaps widened. The gap between HiOECD and middle-income countries increased slightly, from 8.1 to 8.6 years, mainly because life expectancies in middle-income EEFSU nations declined along with their economies while the gap between HiOECD and sub-Saharan Africa increased from 26.4 to 31.2 years, largely due to HIV/AIDS, malaria, and tuberculosis and aggravated by additional economic disruption arising from civil and cross-border conflicts (Goklany 2002a, 11).

Increases in the life expectancy gap in the 1990s occurred because when faced with new diseases (for example, AIDS) or a resurgence of ancient ones (for example, malaria and tuberculosis), poor countries lacked the economic and human resources to develop effective treatments or to import and adapt treatments invented and developed in rich countries. In other words, although the technologies are out there to cure many diseases, poor countries cannot afford them. This unfortunate state of affairs exists not only for expensive-to-treat diseases (for example, AIDS), but also for diseases that are relatively cheap to treat (for example, tuberculosis and malaria). Although neither globalization nor wealth are ends in themselves, globalization increases wealth, which in turn advances more direct measures of human well-being by providing the resources to improve these measures (see Chapter 4, by B. Delworth Gardner, in this book).

Regardless of whether globalization has increased income inequality, gaps between rich and poor in the more critical measures of human well-being have shrunk dramatically since the mid-1900s. Notably, where these gaps in well-being have shrunk the least or even expanded in recent years, it is because of too little, rather than too much, globalization.

Finally, the rich are not better off because they have taken something from the poor, rather the poor are better off because they have benefited from the technologies developed by the rich; their situation would have improved further had they been better able to capture the benefits of globalization. In fact, if the rich can be faulted at all, it is that by subsidizing favored economic sectors and maintaining import barriers, they have retarded globalization and made it harder for many developing countries to capture its benefits.

The Cycle of Progress

We have seen that human welfare advanced more during the twentieth century than it had in all the rest of mankind's tenure on Earth. This progress in human well-being was sustained, and perhaps even initiated, by a cycle composed of the mutually reinforcing, coevolving forces of economic growth, technological change, and free trade.

Technology increases food production through various mechanisms. It boosts yields through special seeds, mechanization, judicious application of inputs such as fertilizers and lime, and reductions of losses to pests, spoilage, and waste. Use of this technology is closely linked to economic development because not everyone can afford it. One reason poorer countries have lower cereal yields is that farmers cannot afford sufficient fertilizer and other yield-enhancing technologies (Goklany 1998, 2000). Thus yields increase over time and with wealth (Goklany 2001a, 26).

More food also means more healthy people who are less likely to succumb to infectious and parasitic diseases. That—along with capital and human resources targeted on improvements in medicine and public health—has reduced mortality and increased life expectancy worldwide (Fogel 1995, 2000; World Health Organization 1999). Hence, as populations become more affluent, mortality decreases and life expectancy increases (Goklany 1999b; see also Pritchett and Summers 1996; World Bank 1993). Thus, a wealthier population is healthier.

A healthier population also is wealthier because it is more productive (Barro 1997; Bloom 1999; Fogel 1995; World Bank 1993; World Health Organization 1999). Fogel (1995, 65) estimates that the level of food supplies in eighteenth-century France was so low that the bottom 10 percent of the labor force could not generate the energy needed for regular work, and the next 10 percent had enough energy for about half an hour of heavy work (or less than three hours of light work).

A healthier and longer-lived population also is likely to invest more time and effort in developing its human capital, which contributes to the creation and diffusion of technology. It is not surprising that levels of education have gone up with life expectancy or that researchers today spend what at one period was literally a lifetime to acquire skills and expertise necessary for a career in research.

In addition, several measures undertaken to improve public health provided a bonus in economic productivity. Draining swamps not only reduced malaria but also added to the agricultural land base (Easterlin 1996). World Bank (1993, 19) reported that an international program to curtail river blindness, the Onchocersiasis Control Program, a mixture of drug therapy and insecticide spraying, has protected thirty million people (including nine million children) from the disease, and it is freeing up 25 million hectares (60 million acres) of land for cultivation and settlement. The improved food supplies should result in better nutrition, which may aid learning. (This is one of the premises behind school meals programs [Watkins 1997].)

Improvements specific to health, food, and agriculture also benefit from a larger, more general cycle in which broad technological change, economic growth, and global trade reinforce each other. Other technologies—invented for other reasons—have led to medical advances and improved productivity or reduced the environmental impacts of the food and agricultural sector. For example, computers, lasers, and global positioning systems permit precision agriculture to optimize the timing and quantities of fertilizers, water, and pesticides, increasing productivity while reducing environmental impacts. Plastics—essential for food packaging and preservation—also increase productivity of the food and agricultural sector. Transportation of every kind increases the ability to move inputs and outputs from farm to market and from market to farm. Broad advances in physics and engineering have led to new or improved medical technologies, including electricity (without which virtually no present-day hospital or operating room could function), X-rays, nuclear magnetic resonance, lasers, and refrigeration.

These specific impacts do not exhaust the benefits of broad economic growth, technological change, and global trade. Technological change in general reinforces economic growth (Barro 1997; Goklany 1998), giving countries more resources to research and develop technological improvements (Goklany 1995) and to increase education.

Freer trade contributes directly to greater economic growth, helps disseminate new technologies, and creates competitive pressures to invent and innovate (Goklany 1995). As an example, trade accelerated the cleanup of automobile emissions in the United States because the threat of cleaner cars from imports advanced the introduction of catalytic converters in the 1970s (Barbour 1980; Seskin 1978).

By expanding competition, trade helps contain the costs of basic infrastructure, including water supply and sanitation systems. A vivid example of the importance of trade in improving human well-being comes from prewar Iraq. Because of trade sanctions, Iraq was unable to operate and maintain much of its water, sanitation, and electricity systems, resulting in significant public health problems (United Nations 2000).

In terms of income alone, trade raises incomes for both the poor and the rich (Dollar and Kraay 2000a; see also Frankel and Romer 1999). Dollar and Kraay (2000a) also find that economic growth favors rich and poor equally, confirming analyses by Ravallion and Chen (1997) and Easterly and Rebelo (1993). Similarly, increased protection of property rights and fiscal discipline (defined as low government consumption) raise overall incomes without increasing inequality (Dollar and Kraay 2000a).

Thus, each link in the cycle—higher yields, increased food supplies, lower mortalities, and higher life expectancies—is strengthened by the general forces of economic growth, technological change, and trade. Qualitatively at least, this explains why all the figures for cereal yields, food supplies per capita, safe water, life expectancy, and postsecondary education, when plotted against per-capita income (as seen in figures here and in Goklany 2001a), show improvement, with rising per-capita incomes.

Conclusion

The foregoing brief investigation into the course of human well-being since the start of industrialization reinforces Lomborg's (2001) conclusion that the state of humanity has never been better (87, 328). For every indicator of human well-being examined in this chapter, cross-country analysis shows that well-being advances with the level of economic development. These improvements are generally greatest at the lowest levels of economic development. This gives further credence to

Lomborg's contention that economic development is a key factor in advancing well-being (324, 327).

This chapter also extends Lomborg's analysis by showing explicitly that technological change is critical to such advances. Thus, Lomborg is justified in his skepticism of a precautionary principle that would— under the cover of the old aphorism "better safe than sorry"—limit new technologies if, despite clear and certain social, economic, or health-related benefits, they also might result in uncertain environmental costs (348–50; Goklany 2001b, 2002b). Calling such an approach a "precautionary principle" would be a misnomer; it would prolong existing risks to human well-being and, thereby, retard further progress. Perhaps the most vivid examples of the perverse outcomes of such misuse of the principle are Zambia's rejection of genetically modified maize to feed its starving population, and the discontinuation of spraying DDT indoors in areas where that effectively reduces malaria (Goklany 2001b). In order to ensure that the precautionary principle does indeed reduce overall risk, decisions regarding new technologies must weigh the social, public health, and environmental benefits against the costs associated with adopting (or rejecting) those technologies (Goklany 2002b).

The importance of both technological change and economic development is reinforced by trends in gaps in well-being in the past half-century. During the first two decades of that period, gaps in some well-being indicators between rich and poor countries shrank, although inequalities in income, that is, economic development, increased. The shrinkage was because of technological change brought about by the diffusion of technologies from the rich to the poor via trade in and transfer of goods, ideas, knowledge, and services, that is, through globalization. More recently, however, gaps in life expectancy between the rich countries and sub-Saharan Africa and EEFSU nations have begun to expand. This is largely because of economic difficulties in these areas, which rendered them unable to marshal the resources needed to acquire and implement the technologies for dealing with new diseases (for example, AIDS) or the resurgence of old diseases (for example, tuberculosis and malaria). Thus, despite the vociferous complaints one hears about globalization, insufficient globalization creates a larger problem.

Notably, improvements in well-being have not yet run their full course. Substantial additional improvements in infant mortality and life expectancy are possible in developing countries if they become wealthier and if existing-but-underused safe-water, sanitation, and agricultural technologies are more widely spread (Lomborg 2001, 334–35). However, once the easy and relatively cheap improvements in health and life expectancy have been captured, solutions to remaining problems (such as AIDS and the diseases of affluence), being expensive, might be increasingly unaffordable, whether one lives in a developed or developing country. Further improvements in human well-being will depend largely on the development of human and capital resources and encouraging the development and deployment of new risk-reduction technologies. Thus, it is critical to focus on strengthening the domestic and international institutions that will boost technological change and economic development, which include free markets, freer trade, individual property rights, the rule of law, and transparent government and bureaucracies.

Notes

1. For hunger, see Lomborg (2001) at 60–62; education, 80–82; wealth, 70–71; health as measured by infant mortality, 53–55; life expectancy, 50–53.
2. The logarithm of per-capita income is used to moderate the impact on the index from additional increases in income.
3. This is the first of several curves plotting various indicators against GDP per capita (in 1995 U.S. dollars at market exchange rates, MXR). To better illustrate the dependence of indicators at low- to mid-levels of economic development, the scales for this and similar figures are cut off at mid-levels of GDP per capita. Unless noted otherwise, the smoothed curves in all these figures were generated using log-linear relationships, and the slopes, that is, the coefficients of the log (GDP per capita) term, are significant ($p < 0.001$). In Figure 2.1, for 1961, the number of observations (N) was

92, and $R^2 = 0.61$. For 1994, $N = 150$ and $R^2 = 0.63$. Also, unless otherwise noted, the shifts in the indicator as we go from one year to the other, that is, the y-intercepts, are also significant ($p < 0.001$). This shift informs us about the effect of technology over time in the level of the indicator. According to the regression analyses, if per-capita income had been frozen at \$300 (in 1995 U.S. dollars, MXR), available food supplies would have increased from 2,004 calories per capita per day in 1961 to 2,148 calories per capita per day in 1994.

4. N and R^2 for 1962 and 1997 are 96 and 0.71 and 148 and 0.65, respectively. If per capita income had been frozen at \$300 (in 1995 U.S. dollars), life expectancy would have increased from 44.7 years in 1962 to 55.0 in 1997. Also see note 1.

5. Dollars for United States, China, and India are all adjusted for purchasing power parity (Maddison 1995 and 1999).

6. The curves in Figure 2.3 were fitted using a log-log relationship. N and R^2 for 1962 and 1997 were 96 and 0.71 and 147 and 0.79, respectively. The significant lowering of the curve over time is consistent with the creation and diffusion of new and existing-but-underused technologies. If GDP per capita had been frozen at \$300 (in 1995 U.S. dollars), infant mortality rate would have declined from 147 per 1,000 live births in 1962 to 82 in 1997. Also see note 1.

7. International dollars are obtained using a special conversion factor, purchasing power parity, designed to reflect more accurately the purchasing powers of different currencies. Conversion is based on the number of units of a country's currency required to buy the same amounts of goods and services in the domestic market as \$1 would buy in the United States. In contrast, the market exchange rate (MXR) of a currency in U.S. dollars (used elsewhere in this chapter) is the amount of the currency one can buy with one U.S. dollar on the open currency market.

8. Ausubel and Grubler define "disposable" life hours as the average hours in a lifetime minus: (a) the hours equivalent to ten years to account for childhood and basic elementary education, and (b) the hours needed to take care of basic physiological needs such as eating, sleeping, and basic hygiene.

9. N and R^2 for 1965 and 1996 were 82 and 0.54 and 137 and 0.64, respectively. The increases in the intercepts, which are significant, are probably due to increasing knowledge about the benefits of education and the willingness and ability of families and societies to incur the costs of longer

periods of education. Globally, postsecondary enrollment increased from 6.8 percent in 1965 to 18.8 percent in 1996. Also see note 1.

10. As noted previously, the index uses the logarithm of GDP per capita.

References

Ausubel, J. H., and A. Grübler. 1995. Working less and living longer. *Technological Forecasting and Social Change* 50: 113–31.

Barney, Gerald O., ed. 1980. The global 2000 report to the president of the U.S.: Entering the twenty-first century. New York: Pergamon Press.

Barbour, I. G. 1980. *Technology, environment, and human values.* New York: Praeger.

Barro, R. J. 1997. *The determinants of economic growth: A cross-country empirical study.* Cambridge, Mass.: MIT Press.

Becker, Charles, and David Bloom. 1998. The demographic crisis in the former Soviet Union: Introduction. *World Development* 26: 1913–19.

Bloom, Barry R. 1999. The future of public health. *Nature* 402 (supplement): C63–64.

Brown, Lester R. 1998. The future of growth. In *The state of the world 1998*, ed. Brown, Lester R., Christopher Flavin, and Hilary F. French. New York: W. W. Norton, 3–20.

Bureau of the Census. 1975. *Historical statistics of the United States, colonial times to 1970.* Washington, D.C.: Government Printing Office.

———. 1999. Statistical abstract of the United States, 1999. Washington, D.C.: Government Printing Office.

Burnette, J., and J. Mokyr. 1995. The standard of living through the ages. In *The state of humanity,* ed. Julian L. Simon. Cambridge, Mass.: Blackwell, 135–48.

Dollar, David, and Aart Kraay. 2000a. *Growth is good for the poor.* Transition Newsletter. World Bank, Development Economics Research Group. Online: http://www.worldbank.org/research/growth/absdollakray.htm.

———. 2000b. Spreading the wealth. *Foreign Affairs,* (January–February). Online: http://www.foreignaffairs.org/articles/Dollar0102.html. Cited May 26, 2002.

Easterlin, Richard A. 1996. *Growth triumphant: The twenty-first century in historical perspective.* Ann Arbor: University of Michigan Press.

Easterly, William, and Sergio T. Rebelo. 1993. Fiscal policy and economic

Growth: An empirical investigation. *Journal of Monetary Economics* 32 (3): 417–58.

Ehrlich, Paul R. 1968. *The population bomb*. New York: Ballantine Books.

Fogel, R. W. 1995. The contribution of improved nutrition to the decline of mortality rates in Europe and America. In *The state of humanity*, ed. Julian L. Simon. Cambridge, Mass.: Blackwell, 61–71.

———. 2000. *The fourth great awakening and the future of egalitarianism.* Chicago: University of Chicago Press.

Food and Agricultural Organization (FAO). 1996a. Assessment of feasible progress in food security. Technical Background Documents 12–15, vol. 3. Rome.

FAO. 1996b. The state of food and agriculture. Rome.

———. 1999. The state of food insecurity in the world 1999. December. Online: http://www.fao.org/FOCUS/E/aSOFI/home-e.htm.

———. 2000. FAOStat. Online: http://apps.fao.org.

———. 2003. FAOStat. Online: http://apps.fao.org.

Frankel, Jeffrey A., and David Romer. 1999. Does trade cause growth? *American Economic Review* (June): 379–99.

Goklany, Indur M. 1995. Strategies to enhance adaptability: Technological change, sustainable growth and free trade. *Climatic Change* 30: 427–49.

———. 1998. Saving habitat and conserving bio-diversity on a crowded planet. *BioScience* 48: 941–53.

———. 1999a. *Clearing the air: The real story of the war on air pollution.* Washington, D.C.: Cato Institute.

———. 1999b. The future of industrial society. Paper presented at the International Conference on Industrial Ecology and Sustainability, University of Technology of Troyes, Troyes, France, September 22–25. Available from author, Office of Policy Analysis, Dept. of the Interior, 1849 C St. NW, Washington, D.C. 20240.

———. 1999c. Meeting global food needs: The environmental trade-offs between increasing land conversion and land productivity. *Technology* 6: 107–30.

———. 2000. Potential consequences of increasing atmospheric CO_2 concentration compared to other environmental problems. *Technology* 7S: 189–213.

———. 2001a. Economic growth and the state of humanity. *PERC Policy Series* PS-21. Bozeman, Mont.: PERC.

————. 2001b. *The precautionary principle: A critical appraisal of environmental risk assessment*. Washington, D.C.: Cato Institute.

————. 2002a. *The globalization of human well-being*. Policy Analysis 447. Washington, D.C.: Cato Institute.

————. 2002b. From precautionary principle to risk-risk analysis. *Nature Biotechnology* 20: 1075.

Gwartney, James, Randall Holcombe, and Robert Lawson. 1998. The scope of government and the wealth of nations. *Cato Journal* 18: 163–90.

Gwartney, James, Robert Lawson, and D. Samida. 2000. *Economic freedom of the world 2000*. Vancouver, B.C.: Fraser Institute.

Hill, K. 1995. The decline in childhood mortality. In *The State of Humanity*, ed. Julian L. Simon. Cambridge, Mass.: Blackwell, 37–50.

Lee, J., and W. Feng. 1999. Malthusian models and Chinese realities: The Chinese demographic system, 1700–2000. *Population and Development Review* 25: 33–65.

Lomborg, Bjørn. 2001. *The skeptical environmentalist: Measuring the real state of the world*. New York: Cambridge University Press.

Maddison, A. 1995. *Monitoring the world economy, 1820–1992*. Paris: OECD.

————. 1998. *Chinese economic performance in the long run*. Paris: OECD.

————. 1999. Poor until 1820. *Wall Street Journal*, January 11, millennium edition, R54.

Mitchell, B. R. 1992. *International historical statistics: Europe, 1750–1988*. New York: Stockton Press.

Mitchell, D. O., and M. D. Ingco. 1993. The world food outlook. *Hunger Notes* 19 (Winter 1993–1994): 20–25.

Paddock, W., and P. Paddock. 1967. *Famine 1975! America's decision: Who will survive?* Boston: Little, Brown.

Preston, S. H. 1995. Human mortality throughout history and prehistory. In *The State of Humanity*, ed. Julian L. Simon. Cambridge, Mass.: Blackwell, 30–36.

Pritchett, Lant, and Lawrence H. Summers. 1996. Wealthier is healthier. *Journal of Human Resources* 31: 841–68.

Ravallion, Martin, and Shaohua Chen. 1997. What can new survey data tell us about recent changes in distribution and poverty? *World Bank Economic Review* 11 (2): 357–82.

Sala-i-Martin, Xavier. 2002. The world distribution of income (estimated from individual country distributions). Online: http://www.columbia.edu/~xs23/papers/pdfs/WorldIncomeDistribution.pdf.

Seskin, E. P. 1978. Automobile air pollution policy. In *Current Issues in U.S. Environmental Policy*, ed. Paul Portney. Baltimore, Md.: Johns Hopkins University Press.

Simon, Julian L., ed. 1995. *The State of Humanity*. Cambridge, Mass.: Blackwell.

United Nations. 2000. Security Council extends Iraq "oil-for-food" program for further 186 days. Press release SC/6872. June 8. Online: http://www.un.org/News/Press/docs/2000/20000608.sc6872.doc.html.

United Nations Development Program. 1999. Human development report 1999. New York: Oxford University Press.

————. 2000. Human development report 2000. New York: Oxford University Press.

————. 2001. Human development report 2001. New York: Oxford University Press.

Watkins, Shirley R. 1997. Historical perspective on the school meals programs: The case for strong federal programs. Paper presented at Ceres Forum on School Meals Policy, Georgetown University Center for Food and Nutrition Policy, November 24, Washington, D.C. Online: http://www.fns.usda.gov/fncs/shirley/speeches/support/sw971124.htm.

World Bank. 1993. World development report: Investing in health. New York: Oxford University Press.

————. 1999. World development indicators. CD-ROM. Washington, DC.

————. 2001. World development indicators. CD-ROM. Washington, D.C.

World Health Organization. 1999. The world health report 1999. Geneva, Switzerland.

World Resources Institute. 1998. World resources 1998–99 database. Washington, D.C.

Wrigley, E. A., and R. S. Schofield. 1981. *The population history of England, 1541–1871: A reconstruction*. Cambridge, Mass.: Harvard University Press.

Chapter 3

Income and
the Race
to the Top

Bruce Yandle
Maya Vijayaraghavan
Madhusudan Bhattarai

IN MARCH 2001, Matt Ridley, zoologist, editor, and author of *The Origins of Virtue* (1996), delivered the Prince Phillip Lecture to the Royal Society of Arts in London, an address he titled "Technology and the Environment: The Case for Optimism" (Ridley 2002). Noting that he was convinced that things environmental were getting better, Ridley explained how, in an earlier time, he had been a deep-ecology environmentalist. Like many others, at the time, he believed that the duo of modern technology and unbridled capitalism was the chief source of harm to the environment. As the cause of the problem, these combined forces could never be the solution to modern environmental decay.

Bruce Yandle is professor emeritus of economics at Clemson University and a PERC senior associate; Maya Vijayaraghavan is an economist with the Global Measles Branch, Global Immunization Division at the Centers for Disease Control and Prevention; and Madhusudan Bhattarai is a postdoctoral economist at the International Water Management Institute in Colombo, Sri Lanka. This chapter draws on and uses content from their paper "Environmental Kuznets Curves: A Primer," PERC Research Study RS 02-1 (2002). The authors thank PERC for permission to use content from the earlier report and acknowledge with deep appreciation the editing assistance provided by Jane Shaw. Dr. Vijayaraghavan's research on this paper was undertaken while she was a research associate at Clemson University's Center for International Trade.

Ridley's position on the cause of environmental decay and the prospects for improvement changed fundamentally when he encountered the work of Aaron Wildavsky (1988) and Julian Simon (1981). These two American scholars, more so than any others, were unrelenting in their marshalling of facts and logic demonstrating that the world was getting safer, not riskier, cleaner, not dirtier; that mankind's future would be brighter, not more dismal; and that uncoordinated market forces, not government, would provide the stimulus for delivering a cleaner and richer world. Ridley became convinced that when property rights are enforced under a rule of law, the market works to improve environmental quality.

More recently, the Danish statistician Bjørn Lomborg provided another volume of good cheer for the yet-to-be-persuaded environmental pessimists. Having also encountered Julian Simon's work, Lomborg explains how he, a committed pessimistic environmentalist, changed his position after completing a massive examination of data.[1] His altered position is captured in the title of his book, *The Skeptical Environmentalist: Measuring the Real State of the World* (2001). Lomborg indicates that he deliberately chose a title to serve as counterpoint to the best-selling *State of the World*, a widely read annual publication of the Worldwatch Institute. As he takes the reader through reams of charts and data, Lomborg debunks a number of pessimistic assertions found in the Worldwatch publication. Where Ridley's conversion was based primarily on theory and logic, Lomborg's transformation was based on cold hard facts.

Lomborg and Ridley join a growing list of author-scientists who report good news about the modern search for improved environmental quality. Instead of somehow being caught in a never-ending race to the bottom where, in the name of keeping and attracting industry, each community accepts more pollution than its neighbor, people of the industrialized and developing worlds alike are engaging in what might be called a race to the top. But it is a peculiar race, one in which— barring takeover by despots, natural disasters, and destruction that can

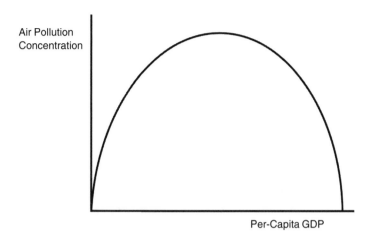

Figure 3.1   Environmental Kuznets Curve

be unleashed by holy and unholy wars—all contestants win. There are no obvious losers. The race has to do with building a better life with the same amount of resource utilization, or even less. When structured around property rights and the rule of law, it is a positive-sum game involving natural resource management and environmental improvement in which all participants taken together are made better off.

All this sounds too good to be true. How can it be? How can risks be reduced, environmental quality improved, endangered species given more protection, forests be better managed, and income increased so that all are made better off? When it is clear that many dimensions of environmental quality are improving, explaining how this has happened is indeed the challenge.

This chapter is about the evidence that incomes can increase and environmental quality can improve simultaneously. It is about environmental Kuznets curves (EKCs), those statistical artifacts that map relationships between a community's income and some specific measure of environmental quality, such as concentrations of sulfur dioxide at particular locations. A general-form EKC is shown in Figure 3.1. For illustrative purposes, the EKC shows a relationship between per-capita gross domestic product (GDP) and concentrations of a specific air pollutant.

An in-depth discussion of the general shape and what we know about EKCs comes later, but for now the point needs to be made that there is a human story that lies behind any observed EKC. It is this: Rising incomes enable human communities to build advanced property rights institutions that limit environmental decay and reward environmental improvement. The race to the top, which is that part of an EKC that shows environmental improvement accompanying income increases, is about escaping the commons and building fences. More will be said later about the first part of the curve where the environment deteriorates with rising income.

The chapter is organized as follows: The next section is launched by making quick reference to the idea of Aaron Wildavsky that inspired Lomborg and Ridley, the idea that richer is safer. The section then explains how the income–environmental quality relationship was first discovered and applied in a policy controversy and how that first episode of discovery inspired a host of EKC investigations. The results of these investigations are summarized.

But, of course, institutional change lies behind the observed correlation. Humankind is an institution builder. If new institutions are to emerge, older ones must be displaced. A process of creative destruction takes place when resources are conserved.[2] Institutional change and property rights are made part of the EKC discussion in the second section. The last section provides some final thoughts on the EKC relationship.

Richer Is Safer and Cleaner

One part of the inverted U-shaped environmental Kuznets curve emphasizes Aaron Wildavsky's (1988) point, that richer is safer and cleaner. Another part of the EKC, that which maps very low incomes to a measure of environmental quality, implies just the reverse: Richer is riskier and dirtier. But although we can observe what might be called the "race to the bottom" exemplified in the first part of the EKC, we just as readily see the portion that describes "the race to the top." As Wildavsky understood it, those societies that engage in wealth creation at some point become engaged in selective environmental improvement. No, not every dimension of life that someone might term environmental will be improved; reflected in the EKC are only those environmental elements that are seen as being worthy of the cost of protecting and enhancing by the people who make the decision and bear the cost. It should be emphasized that the structure of property rights institutions has a lot to do with who decides and who bears the cost. If property rights ownership is decentralized and private citizens gain and lose on the basis of environmental decisions, then public and private parties who make environmental decisions will be conditioned by private property rights.

Improving the environment is not free; opportunity costs matter to real people. How it happens is a story about growing incomes and environmental use. But it is not just a story about income and the environment. Income increases alone will not bring changes in environmental quality. Rising incomes become the means for making institutional changes that will conserve and, in some cases, rebuild environmental quality. Income-driven institutional change is costly, but not as costly as an unbounded tragedy of the commons.

Early EKC Discoveries

Grossman and Krueger (1991) were the first to model the relationship between environmental quality and economic growth. They analyzed the EKC relationship in the context of the much-debated North American Free Trade Agreement. At the time, many people feared that opening markets with Mexico would invite a race to the bottom—companies would try to find the lowest environmental standards they could get away with. Environmentally intensive factories, it was said, would rush across the border to escape the stricter environmental standards of Canada and the United States.

Without saying so, Grossman and Krueger implicitly tested the Wildavsky hypothesis. They proposed that rising incomes from trade would lead to stricter environmental control. In other words, free trade would improve incomes and protect the environment. To address the hypothesis, they developed a cross-country panel of comparable measures of air pollution in various urban areas and explored the relationship between economic growth and air quality. The data for their statistical experiments came from a joint project of the World Health Organization and the United Nations Environment Programme that began in 1976. The Global Environmental Monitoring System (GEMS) has as its goal the improvement of air-quality monitoring in urban areas worldwide. GEMS monitors air quality in cities around the world on a daily, weekly, or less frequent basis.[3] In all, forty-two countries are represented in Grossman and Krueger's sample for sulfur dioxide, nineteen countries for smoke or dark matter, and twenty-nine for suspended particulates. The participating cities are located in a variety of developing and developed countries and were chosen to roughly represent the world's different geographic conditions. In most of the cities, air quality measurements are taken at two or three different sites, which are classified as center city or suburban and as commercial, industrial, or residential. Multiple sites in the same city are monitored because pollutant concentrations can vary dramatically with local conditions and land use.

Grossman and Krueger held constant the identifiable geographic characteristics of different cities, a common global time trend in the levels of pollution, and the location and type of the pollution measurement device. With these constant, they found that ambient levels of both sulfur dioxide and dark matter (smoke) suspended in the air increase with per-capita GDP at low levels of national income, but decrease with per-capita GDP at higher levels of income. These findings provided statistical evidence for the existence of an EKC relationship for two indicators of environmental quality. The turning point came for sulfur dioxide and smoke when per-capita GDP was in the range of $4,000 to $5,000 in 1985 US$ (or about $6,200 to $8,200 in 2001). Unlike the relationship found for sulfur dioxide and smoke, no turning point was found for the mass of suspended particulate matter in a given volume of air. In this case, the relationship between pollution and GDP was monotonically increasing.[4] Based on revealed behavior, sulfur dioxide and smoke emissions mattered more to the populations in the study than suspended particulate matters. On the basis of health risks, the people in the study areas seem to have gotten it right.

Following closely on the heels of the Grossman and Krueger study, Shafik and Bandopadhyay (1992) estimated the relationship between economic growth and several key indicators of environmental quality reported in the World Bank's cross-country time-series data sets.[5] They found a consistently significant relationship between income and all indicators of environmental quality they examined. As income increases from low levels, quantities of sulfur dioxide, suspended particulate matter, and fecal coliform increase initially, then decrease once the economy reaches a certain level of income. The turning-point incomes in 1985 US$ for these pollutants are $3,700, $3,300 and $1,400 respectively.[6] (In 2001 US$, the turning points would be about $6,100, $5,400, and $2,300).

Does Cleaner in Some Places
Mean Dirtier Elsewhere?

The early EKC discoveries naturally raised a question about globalization. Does a race to the top in higher-income countries mean that dirty industries are exported, causing an early race to the bottom in developing countries? In a 1992 study, Hettige, Lucas, and Wheeler explored the EKC phenomenon further and indirectly addressed this question. They developed a production toxic intensity index for thirty-seven manufacturing sectors in eighty countries over the period 1960 to 1988.[7] Their goal was to avoid focusing on individual measures of environmental quality, such as air quality, and to instead generalize the environmental impact of manufacturing by determining if manufacturing became more or less "toxic" in relation to income. The index, based on information from the U.S. Environmental Protection Agency and the U.S. Census of Manufacturers, attempted to measure a country's toxicity, or pollution intensity. The researchers could then identify the extent to which polluting production did or did not shift from higher- to lower-income countries when incomes rose faster in one than the other.

The results of the study indicate the existence of an EKC relationship for toxic intensity per unit of GDP. No evidence, however, was found for toxic intensity measured per unit of manufacturing output. When the mix of manufacturing was held constant, Hettige, Lucas, and Wheeler found that manufacturing in low-income countries was not more toxic, nor was manufacturing in high-income countries less toxic. Manufacturing, which is just one part of GDP, did not become cleaner or dirtier as income changed. Instead, manufacturing became smaller relative to services and trade in expanding economies. This suggests that higher income leads to a demand for a cleaner environment regardless of whether the environment has been damaged by a toxic-producing manufacturing sector. The authors conclude that the GDP-based intensity result is due solely to a broad shift away from industry and toward lower-polluting services as development proceeds.

This could mean that dirty production shifts elsewhere. To examine whether this happened, the authors divided the data into subsets for each decade beginning with 1960. They found the estimated pattern for the 1960s to be quite different from that of later decades. For the 1960s, toxic intensity grew most quickly in high-income economies. This pattern was sharply reversed during the 1970s and 1980s, when toxic intensity in manufacturing in less-developed countries grew most quickly. What might explain the shift to these countries?

The authors extended their analysis to investigate the possibility that toxic displacement has been affected by the trade policies of less-developed countries. Their investigation indicates that the toxic intensity of manufacturing output in these countries rises when governments protect their chemical manufacturing sector with tariffs and nontariff trade barriers. They also find that less-developed countries that are outward-oriented and high-growth have slow-growing or even declining toxic intensities of manufacturing, whereas toxic intensity increases more rapidly in inward-oriented economies—those with less trade.

The Hettige, Lucas, and Wheeler findings on trade policy and toxic intensity suggest a revised view of the displacement phenomenon, or "pollution-haven," theory. Rapidly increasing toxic intensity does not seem to characterize all manufacturing in less developed countries in the 1970s, when environmental regulation in industrialized countries became more strict. Rather, toxic intensity in manufacturing has grown much more rapidly in economies that are relatively closed to international trade. Goklany (2001) emphasizes this point, which Grossman and Krueger (1991) also note: Open economies improve their environments. More open economies have had higher growth rates of labor-intensive assembly activities that are also relatively low in toxic intensity. Highly protected economies have had more rapid growth of capital-intensive smokestack sectors. A market-based property-rights theory predicts that when ordinary people have the right to trade and to hold polluters accountable, then open markets can lead to a cleaner outcome. Additional evidence on this point is found in the work of Suri and Chapman (1998). Their findings imply that global diffusion of manufacturing contributes to environmental improvements as incomes rise and development continues.

What About Trees?

An EKC study by Cropper and Griffiths (1994) moved away from pollution to study deforestation. Cropper and Griffiths examined the effect of population pressures on deforestation in sixty-four developing countries. Income and population growth are the factors underlying the rate of deforestation in their study. Since deforestation is primarily a problem of developing countries, the authors restricted their study to non-OECD (Organisation for Economic Co-operation and Development) countries in Africa, Asia, and Latin America roughly located in the tropical belt and with a forest area of more than 1,000,000 hectares. The results were uncertain for Asia owing partly to the small amount of variation in the data, according to the authors. They discovered the inverted U EKC for the Latin America and Africa samples. However, the per-capita income levels in most countries in Latin America and Africa were to the left of (lower than) the respective peaks ($5,420 and $4,760) of their estimated EKCs. The inference could still be drawn that, for countries on these two continents, as income increases the rate of deforestation levels off.

In another 1995 study, Panayotou investigated the EKC relationship for deforestation, sulfur dioxide, oxides of nitrogen, and suspended particulate matter. He used mid- to late-1980s data from forty-one tropical, mostly developing countries for deforestation, and late 1980s data for fifty-five countries (both developed and developing) for emissions of sulfur dioxide and oxides of nitrogen. The findings indicate that the turning-point income for deforestation is earlier than the turning point for emissions. Panayotou argued that environmental degradation overall (combined resource depletion and pollution) is worse at levels of income per capita under $1,000 (in 1985 US$). Between $1,000 and $3,000, both the economy and environmental degradation undergo a dramatic structural change, from rural to urban and from the principal pursuit of agricultural production to industrial production. He noted that a second structural transformation begins to take place as countries surpass a per-capita income of $10,000 and begin to shift from energy-intensive heavy industry into services and information-intensive industries.

Replicating and Updating Earlier Studies

Selden and Song (1994) examined the two air pollutants studied by Grossman and Krueger, along with oxides of nitrogen and carbon monoxide. They used GEMS data across countries and across time to model the relationship between per-capita GDP and the air pollutants.[8] Broadly speaking, their results lend support to the existence of an EKC relationship for all four air pollutants. The EKC turning point (in 1985 US$) for sulfur dioxide was nearly $9,000 and in the vicinity of $10,000 for suspended particulate matter. (In 2001 US$, the figures would be about $14,500 and $16,400.) Both figures are significantly higher than the estimates from Grossman and Krueger.

Seldon and Song attribute the higher turning points in their results to their use of aggregate air-quality data, which include readings from both rural and urban areas, rather than the exclusively urban data used by Grossman and Krueger, who expect urban air quality to improve before aggregate data reveal improvement. The turning point for income Seldon and Song found for oxides of nitrogen was above $10,000, while carbon monoxide peaked when income levels were just above $15,000 (or approximately $16,400 and $24,600 in 2001 US$).

In her approach to EKC modeling, Shafik (1994) expanded the variables considered. She hypothesized that there are four determinants of environmental quality in any country: (1) endowment, such as climate or location; (2) per-capita income, which reflects the structure of production, urbanization, and consumption patterns of private goods, including private environmental goods and services; (3) exogenous factors, such as technology, that are available to all countries, but change over time; and (4) policies that reflect social decisions about the provision of environmental public goods' depending on institutions and the sum of individual benefits relative to the sum of individuals' willingness to pay. Shafik then focused on the availability of clean water, access to urban sanitation, ambient levels of suspended particulate matter, ambient levels of sulfur oxides, changes in forest area between 1961 and

1986, the annual rate of deforestation between 1962 and 1986, dissolved oxygen in rivers, fecal coliforms in rivers, municipal waste per capita, and carbon emissions per capita.[9] Shafik's results were mixed. She found an EKC relationship between per-capita income and sulfur dioxide and suspended particulate concentrations. However, the general EKC shape did not hold for carbon emissions per capita, dissolved oxygen in rivers, or forestation/deforestation. Shafik reasons that human populations worry first about access to safe drinking water. In her view, concerns about air pollution arise much later when income growth tends to be associated with manufacturing and energy production. When the link between environmental benefits and disposal costs are not well established, as when solid waste is disposed of in rapidly flowing rivers and there are no downstream rights holders, the Kuznets curve fails to appear. She also takes into account in her estimates technological change and offers an optimistic assessment of how improvements in technology will lead to even faster environmental repair.

Consolidating the Turning Point Data

By the mid-1990s, investigations of EKC relationships had generated enough consistent findings to give assurance that for many pollutants, richer is cleaner. As more and more environmental data were being gathered systematically, it was now possible for researchers to probe even deeper. Having initiated the EKC enterprise, Grossman and Krueger (1995) went back to the drawing board and conducted a more extensive empirical project. Once again, they modeled the relationship between per-capita income and environmental quality using GEMS data sets. Except this time, although they repeated an analysis of air quality, they focused heavily on water quality.

The GEMS/Water project monitors various dimensions of water quality in river basins, lakes, and groundwater aquifers, but the data on lakes and groundwater are quite limited. Because of this, Grossman and Krueger focused their attention on river basins.[10] Their 1995 study

Table 3.1
EKC Turning Points: Grossman and Krueger Analysis

Pollutant	EKC Turning Point (in 1985 US$)	(approx. value in 2001 US$)
Arsenic	$4,900	$8,000
Biological oxygen demand	7,600	12,500
Cadmium	5,000	8,200
Chemical oxygen demand	7,900	13,000
Dissolved oxygen	2,700	4,400
Fecal coliform	8,000	13,100
Nitrates	2,000	3,300
Lead	10,500	17,200
Smoke	6,200	10,200
Sulfur dioxide	4,100	6,700
Total coliform	3,000	4,900

Source: Grossman and Krueger (1995) and authors' calculations

makes use of all variables that can be considered indicators of water quality, provided that they have anthropogenic constituents (not just "natural" pollutants) and that at least ten countries are represented in the sample. They found an EKC relationship for eleven of the fourteen indicators selected for the analysis. The estimated turning-point incomes (in 1985 US$) are shown in Table 3.1.

At this point in EKC research, it is clear that human communities assign a higher priority to improving certain dimensions of water quality than to improving air quality. The evidence is that the income turning points for levels of dissolved oxygen and total coliform in water are lower than for sulfur dioxide, smoke, and suspended particulates in the air. Most likely, the behavior reflects the fact that harms from contaminated water occur much more swiftly and therefore are more clearly visible than those associated with air pollution.

A final piece to be considered in the review of consolidated estimates is that of Cole, Rayner, and Bates (1997). They examined the

relationship between per-capita income and a wide range of environmental indicators using cross-country panel data sets. The environmental indicators used in this analysis are: carbon dioxide, carbonated
fluorocarbons (CFCs) and halons, methane, nitrogen dioxide, sulfur
dioxide, suspended particulates, carbon monoxide, nitrates, municipal
waste, energy consumption, and traffic volumes. Data for the years 1970
through 1992 cover ten OECD countries for nitrogen dioxide, eleven
for sulfur dioxide, seven for suspended particulate matter and carbon
monoxide, nine for nitrogen dioxide and sulfur dioxide from transport,
seven for suspended particulate matter from transport, and twenty-four
for traffic volumes. Data for concentration of nitrates covers the years
1975 through 1990 for thirty rivers in fifteen OECD countries. Carbon
dioxide data are for seven regions between the years 1960 and 1991.

Data on global emissions and total energy use are for twenty-two
OECD countries between 1980 and 1992. CFCs and halons data
include 1986 data for thirty-eight countries and 1990 data for thirty-
nine countries. Late-1980s data were used for methane emissions in
eighty-eight countries and for municipal waste in thirteen OECD countries. Energy use from transport covered twenty-four OECD countries
from 1970 to 1990. In addition, emissions of nitrogen dioxide, sulfur
dioxide, and suspended particulates from the transport sector are considered separately. The range of meaningful turning points estimated
by Cole, Rayner, and Bates (in 1985 US$) are shown in Table 3.2.

Introducing Property Rights
and the Rule of Law

In 1997, a new approach to the EKC relationship was adopted—an
attempt to incorporate explicit policy considerations. Panayotou (1997)
studied the EKC relationship for sulfur dioxide both to gain a better
understanding of the income-environment relationship and as a basis
for conscious policy intervention. Panayotou found that faster economic
growth and higher population density do moderately increase the envi-

Table 3.2
Consolidated Turning Points: Cole, Rayner, and Bates Estimates

Pollutant	EKC Turning Point (in 1985 US$)	(approx. value in 2001 US$)
Carbon dioxide	22,500–34,700	37,000–57,000
Carbon monoxide	9,900–10,100	16,300–16,600
Nitrates	15,600–25,000	25,600–41,000
Nitrogen oxide industrial	14,700–15,100	24,100–24,800
Nitrogen oxide transport	15,100–17,600	24,800–28,900
Sulfur dioxide	5,700– 6,900	9,400–11,300
Sulfur dioxide transport	9,400– 9,800	15,400–16,100
Suspended particulates nontransport	7,300– 8,100	12,000–13,000
Suspended particulates transport	15,000–18,000	24,600–29,600

Source: Cole, Rayner, and Bates (1997) and authors' calculations

ronmental price of economic growth, but better policies can offset these effects and make economic growth more environmentally friendly and sustainable. The sample used in the study includes thirty developed and developing countries for the period 1982 through 1994. The country median of annual sulfur dioxide concentrations was the average of all daily observations obtained from the GEMS air-quality monitoring project.

Proxies for the quality of institutions are used as variables in the study. Panayatou experimented with a set of five indicators of the quality of institutions in general: respect or enforcement of contracts, efficiency of the bureaucracy, the efficacy of the rule of law, the extent of government corruption, and the risk of appropriation, all obtained from Knack and Keefer (1995). Because all these variables were highly correlated, the author chose to use just one of the indicators, the respect or enforcement of contracts. Panayatou's main finding is that the quality of a country's policies and institutions can significantly reduce environmental degradation at low income levels and speed up improvements at higher income levels. Policies such as more secure property rights under

a rule of law and better enforcement of contracts and effective environmental regulations can help flatten the EKC and reduce the environmental price of higher economic growth. The results showing a strong
relationship between property rights enforcement and environmental
quality are consistent with findings by Seth W. Norton (see Chapter 5
of this book).

Following in the footsteps of Panayotou, Qin (1998) included property rights considerations when he estimated EKCs for two common
measures of environmental quality, sulfur dioxide emissions and levels
of dissolved oxygen in rivers. Along with the two traditionally shaped
EKCs, Qin also derived a monotonically increasing EKC for carbon
emissions.[11] The proxy variables Qin used for the quality of institutions
is the index of property rights obtained from Business Environmental
Risk Intelligence (BERI) data. These data are provided by the Center
for Institutional Reform and the Informal Sector (IRIS) at the University
of Maryland and Knack and Keefer (1995), and range continuously
from 0 to 4, with a higher score for greater enforceability of laws governing property rights. Contract enforceability measures the relative
degree to which contractual agreements are honored and complications
presented by language and mentality differences are mitigated.

Qin found the turning-point income for sulfur dioxide to be $7,798
in 1985 purchasing-power-parity-adjusted dollars (about $12,800 in
2001 US$.) The property-rights variable was significant and corre-
sponded to a flatter EKC as the index rose. The estimated turning-point
income for dissolved oxygen in rivers was $3,249 per-capita GDP in
1985 purchasing-power-parity-adjusted dollars (about $5,300 in 2001
US$). The results for the property-rights variable were similar to that
of sulfur dioxide, again saying that property-rights enforcement matters.

Using the annual percentage change in forest area between the
years 1972 and 1991 as an indicator of environmental quality, Bhattarai
(2000) analyzed the EKC relationship for tropical deforestation across
sixty-six countries in Latin America, Asia, and Africa. The study quan-
tifies the relationship between deforestation and income, controlling

for political and governing institutions, macroeconomic policy, and demographic factors. The results from his empirical analysis suggest that underlying political and civil liberties and governing institutional factors (that is, the rule of law, quality of the bureaucracy, level of corruption in government, enforcement of property rights) are relatively more important in explaining the process of tropical deforestation in the recent past than other frequently cited factors in the literature—for example, population growth and shifting cultivation. The study suggests that improvements in political institutions and governance and establishment of the rule of law significantly reduce deforestation. In a related way, macroeconomic policies that lead to increased indebtedness and higher black-market premiums on foreign exchange (measures of trade and exchange-rate policies) will increase the process of deforestation.

Goklany (1999) also was interested in the forces underlying changes in pollution, but he took a more direct policy-analysis approach rather than engaging in statistical analysis for the purpose of estimating an EKC. He examined long-term air quality and emissions data for each of the original five traditional "criteria" air pollutants or their precursors in the United States—sulfur dioxide; particulate matter; carbon monoxide; nitrogen oxides; and ozone or one of its precursors, volatile organic compounds and, to a lesser extent, lead. His data covered the period before and after major environmental laws shifted control of air pollution to the federal government.

Specifically, Goklany examined three separate sets of indicators for each air pollutant. The first set consists of national emissions estimates, which are available from 1900 onward for sulfur dioxide, nitrogen oxides, and volatile organic compounds; the second set from 1940 for particulate matter and carbon monoxide; and the third from 1970 for lead. The second set of indicators is composed of outdoor air-quality measurements. These include ambient concentrations in the outdoor air, which are usually better indicators for the environmental, health, social, and economic impacts of air pollution than are total emissions.

Based upon available data, Goklany developed qualitative trends in national air quality for the various pollutants. These were established from 1957 forward for particulate matter, from the 1960s for sulfur dioxide and carbon monoxide, and from the 1970s for ozone/volatile organic compounds and nitrogen oxides.

The final set of indicators consisted of estimates from 1940 to 1990 of residential combustion emissions per occupied household. Those estimates served as crude proxies for indoor air pollutants, which should serve as a better indicator of the public health impact of various air pollutants than outdoor air quality.

Goklany's findings indicate that before society reaches an environmental transition for a specific pollutant—that is, during the early phases of economic and technological development—"the race to the top of the quality of life" may superficially resemble a "race to the bottom"—or a race to relax environmental standards. But once a society gets past the transition, the race to the top of the quality of life begins to look more like a race to the top of environmental quality.

This could, in fact, create a not-in-my-backyard (NIMBY) situation. Goklany suggests that the apparent race to the bottom and the NIMBY effect are two aspects of the same effort to improve the quality of life. During the apparent race to the bottom, people are improving their lives in ways not clearly "environmental"; during the NIMBY phase, they are improving their lives by keeping out polluters because they are unwilling to pay the costs of controlling the pollution. The former occurs before the turning point, whereas the latter occurs after.

Goklany also examined whether the data support the contention that prior to the national control effected by the Clean Air Act Amendments of 1970, there had been little progress in improving air quality and that states had been engaged in a race to the bottom. His findings do not support those claims, which were used to justify the 1970 federalization.

Final Thoughts

Property rights matter, but there is no single EKC that fits all pollutants for all places and times. There are families of relationships and, in many cases, the inverted U–shaped EKC best approximates the link between environmental change and income growth. The indicators for which the EKC relationship seems most plausible are local air pollutants, such as oxides of nitrogen, sulfur dioxide, and particulate matter.

By way of contrast, there is mixed or little evidence to test the EKC hypothesis for water pollution or for gases, such as carbon dioxide. Robert E. McCormick (see Chapter 6 of this book) provides some initial data that carbon emissions follow the EKC pattern, albeit at much higher income levels. The EKC evidence for water pollution is mixed. There is evidence of an inverted U–shaped curve for biological oxygen demand, chemical oxygen demand, nitrates, and some heavy metals (arsenic and cadmium). In most cases, the income threshold for improving water quality is much lower than that for improving air pollution.

The acceptance of the EKC hypothesis for select pollutants has important policy implications. First, the relationship implies a certain inevitability of environmental degradation along a country's development path, especially during the take-off process of industrialization. Second, the EKC hypothesis suggests that as the development process picks up, when a certain level of per-capita income is reached, economic growth helps to undo the damage done in earlier years. If economic growth is good for the environment, policies that stimulate growth (trade liberalization, economic restructuring, and price reform) ought to be good for the environment. However, income growth without institutional reform is not enough. As we have seen, the improvement of the environment with income growth is not automatic, but depends on policies and institutions. GDP growth creates the conditions for environmental improvement by raising the demand for improved environmental quality and makes the resources available for supplying it.

Whether, when, and how environmental quality improvements materialize depends critically on government policies, social institutions, and the completeness and functioning of markets. It is for this reason, among others, that Arrow et al. (1995) emphasize the importance of getting the institutions right in rich and poor countries. Along these lines, Torras and Boyce (1998) argue and show empirically that, all else equal, when ordinary people have political power and civil as well as economic rights, air and water quality improve in richer and poorer countries.

Better policies, such as the removal of distorting subsidies, introduction of more secure property rights over resources, and imposition of pollution taxes, will flatten the underlying EKC and perhaps achieve an earlier turning point. Because market forces will ultimately determine the price of environmental quality, policies that allow market forces to operate are expected to be unambiguously positive. Therefore, the search for meaningful environmental protection is a search for ways to enhance property rights and markets.

Notes

1. Lomborg discusses his encounter with Simon's ideas and the reactions to his book, both positive and negative, in an interview at Competitive Enterprise Institute. See *CEI Update* (2001). Julian Simon's manifesto of optimism spurred Lomborg to prove Simon wrong. Much to Lomborg's surprise, Simon's optimistic assessment was found to be accurate. In short, the data simply would not support the notion that human communities were systematically destroying the natural environment. The good news was more than many committed environmental pessimists could bear. There is now growing evidence that human communities are not involved in some systematic and perpetual race to the bottom where tragedies of the commons are the norms and never the exception. See Goklany (this volume) and Norton (this volume).

2. "Creative destruction" is a term of art first used to describe the essence of capitalism by economist Joseph Schumpeter (1975 [1942]).

3. Daily (or, in some cases, weekly or less frequent) measurements are taken of the concentrations of sulfur dioxide and suspended particulate matter. Data on particulates are collected by different methods, measuring either

the mass of materials in a given volume of air or the concentration of finer, darker matter ("smoke"). The GEMS sample of cities has changed over time. Sulfur dioxide was monitored in forty-seven cities spread over twenty-eight different countries in 1977, fifty-two cities in thirty-two countries in 1982, and twenty-seven cities in fourteen countries in 1988. Measurements of suspended particulates were taken in twenty-seven cities in eleven countries in 1977, thirty-six cities in seventeen countries in 1982, and twenty-six cities in thirteen countries in 1988, while data for dark matter (smoke) are available for eighteen cities in thirteen countries for 1977, thirteen cities in nine countries for 1982, and seven cities in four countries for 1988.

4. Discovering turning points requires a data set that contains per-capita income or GDP that ranges from very low to high levels. Without this range of incomes, one might observe a monotonically rising or falling relationship between pollution concentrations and income rather than a curve. The appropriate range of incomes is not always available for higher-income countries, such as the United States. If an EKC relationship is observed, it will likely be for the rightmost part of the curve, that portion where rising income levels are associated with environmental improvement. This result is found in work by Carson, Jeon, and McCubbin (1997). They used U.S. state-level emissions for seven major air pollutants: greenhouse gases, air toxins, carbon monoxide, nitrogen oxides, sulfur dioxide, volatile organic carbon, and particulate matter less than ten microns in diameter. In their initial analysis, the authors examined the 1990 state-level per-capita emissions for greenhouse gases converted to pounds of equivalent carbon dioxide, air toxics, and point-source emissions of carbon monoxide, oxides of nitrogen, sulfur dioxide, volatile organic carbon, and particulate matter. They found that emissions per capita decrease with increasing per-capita income for all seven major classes of air pollutants. In this respect, their results are consistent with those from country studies that find an EKC. Hilton and Levinson (1998) found a more complete EKC in their work on auto lead oxide emissions across the developed world. There is a related EKC identification problem when data are examined for all countries worldwide. The heterogeneity of the sample makes it extraordinarily difficult to account for institutional differences (see Stern and Common 2001).

5. Most of the variables cited in this paper are included in the environmental data appendix to the *World Development Report 1992* (World Bank 1992). The sample size varied depending on availability of data. Data on lack of safe water were available only for two years, 1975 and 1985 for forty-four

and forty-three countries, respectively, whereas data on lack of urban
sanitation were available for 1980 and 1985 for fifty-five and seventy
countries, respectively. Annual deforestation reflected the yearly change
in the forest area for sixty-six countries between 1962 and 1986. Total
deforestation was the change in forest area between the earliest date for
which substantial data was available, 1961, and the latest date, 1986. Total
deforestation data were available for seventy-seven countries. Data on
dissolved oxygen were available for fifty-seven rivers distributed in twenty-
seven countries for intermittent years between 1979 and 1988. Data on
fecal coliform were available for fifty-two rivers distributed in twenty-five
countries for intermittent years between 1979 and 1988. Data on ambient
levels of sulfur dioxide were available for forty-seven cities distributed in
thirty-one countries for the years 1972 to 1988, and data on ambient levels
of suspended particulate matter were available for forty-eight cities in
thirty-one countries for 1972 to 1988. Data on municipal solid waste per
capita were computed in kilograms, on the basis of available city level
information for thirty-nine countries compiled for the year 1985. Data on
carbon emissions per capita were available for 118 to 153 countries
between 1960 and 1989.

6. Shafik and Bandyopadhyay also explore the impact of political and civil
liberties on environmental quality. They use Gastil indexes that measure
the level of political and civil liberties in their study. The political rights
index measures rights to participate meaningfully in the political process
for 108 to 119 countries for 1973 and from 1975 to 1986 on a scale of one
to seven where lower numbers indicate greater political rights. A high-
ranking country must have a fully operating electoral procedure, usually
with a significant opposition vote. It is likely to have had a recent change
of government from one party to another, an absence of foreign domina-
tion, decentralized political power, and a consensus that allows all segments of the population some power. The index of civil liberties measures
the extent to which people are able to express their opinion openly without
fear of reprisals and are protected in doing so by an independent judiciary.
Though this index reflects rights to organize and demonstrate as well as
freedom of religion, education, travel, and other personal rights, more
weight is given to the expression of political rights. The results indicate
that political and civil liberties have insignificant effects on access to clean
water and sanitation. Greater political and civil liberties are associated
with increases in the annual rate of deforestation, but total deforestation
over the period 1961–1986 was unaffected. River quality (measured by
dissolved oxygen) improves with increased political liberties, but other
measures are insignificant. In the case of local air pollution, more demo-

cratic countries have higher levels of sulfur dioxides. Particulates and municipal solid wastes were not affected by political or civil liberties. Carbon emissions are ambiguous—with a positive sign in the case of civil liberties and a negative sign for political rights. The results for political and civil liberties therefore indicate no clear pattern.

7. For each country and year, Hettige, Lucas, and Wheeler have used U.N. industrial data to calculate shares of total manufactured output for thirty-seven sectors defined on the international standard industrial classification (ISIC). To obtain country-specific toxic-intensity indexes, they multiplied these shares by U.S. sectoral toxic intensities, estimated as total pounds of toxic release per dollar's worth of output. The sectoral intensities have been calculated from a sample of 15,000 U.S. plants that they obtained by merging data from two sources: the U.S. Environmental Protection Agency's (EPA) 1987 Toxic Release Inventory, which provides plant-level release estimates for 320 toxic substances, and the 1987 Census of Manufacturers, which provides plant-level data on output value. They pool the country-specific toxic-intensity indexes with time-series estimates of income per capita to test two broad hypotheses: (1) industrial pollution intensity follows an inverse U-shaped pattern as development proceeds; and (2) environmental regulation in countries that are part of the Organisation for Economic Cooperation and Development (OECD) has significantly displaced toxic industrial production toward less-regulated LDCs (least-developed countries). The rationale for the latter hypothesis is founded on relative production cost. The former is based on the general notion of three stages of industrial development dominated by (1) agro-processing and light assembly, which are (relatively) low in toxic intensity; (2) heavy industry (for example, metals, chemicals, paper), which has high toxic intensity; and (3) high-technology industry (for example, microelectronics, pharmaceuticals), which is again lower in toxic intensity. This is perceived in part as a natural evolution and in part a response to growing pressure for environmental regulation at higher incomes.

8. The GEMS data used in the paper are obtained from the World Resources Institute. There are twenty-two high-income, six middle-income, and two low-income countries in the sample. Clearly, less-developed countries are underrepresented in the sample.

9. Data and countries covered are the same as in Shafik and Bandyopadhyay (1992).

10. In choosing where to locate its monitoring stations, GEMS/Water has given priority to rivers that are major sources of water supply to municipalities, irrigation, livestock, and selected industries. A number of stations

were included to monitor international rivers and rivers discharging into oceans and seas. Again, the project aimed for representative global coverage. The available water data cover the period 1979–1990. By January 1990 the project had the active participation of 287 river stations in fifty-eight different countries. Each such station reports thirteen basic chemical, physical, and microbiological variables, several globally significant pollutants including various heavy metals and pesticides, and a number of site-specific optional variables.

11. The data for sulfur dioxide emissions were from GEMS, and the sample included data from 1981 to 1986 for fourteen countries. From GEMS/Water stations, three three-year aggregated annual median dissolved-oxygen levels in fifteen countries for 1979–1981, 1982–1985, and 1986–1988 were computed. The data for carbon dioxide were taken from *World Resources 1990–91* and are the cross-country annual carbon dioxide emissions from fossil fuel consumption and cement industries in forty-one countries in 1987.

References

Arrow, Kenneth, Bert Bolin, Robert Costanza, Partha Dasgupta, Carl Folke, C. S. Holling, Bengt-Owe Jansson, Simon Levin, Karl-Goran MŠler, Charles Perrings, David Pimentel. 1995. Economic growth, carrying capacity and the environment. *Science* 268 (April): 520–21.

Bhatarrai, Madhusudan 2000. The environmental Kuznets curve for deforestation in Latin America, Africa, and Asia: Macroeconomic and institutional perspectives. Dissertation (December). Clemson, S.C.: Clemson University.

Carson, Richard T., Yongil Jeon, and Donald R. McCubbin. 1997. The relationship between air pollution emissions and income: U.S. data. *Environment and Development Economics* 2 (4): 433–50.

CEI Update. 2001. Q&A with Bjørn Lomborg. 14 (December): 8–9.

Cole, M. A., A. J. Rayner, and J. M. Bates. 1997. The environmental Kuznets curve: An empirical analysis. *Environment and Development Economics* 2 (4): 401–16.

Cropper, Maureen, and Charles Griffiths. 1994. The interaction of population growth and environmental quality. *American Economic Review Papers and Proceedings* 84 (2): 250–54.

Goklany, Indur M. 1999. *Clearing the air: The real story of the war on air pollution.* Washington, D.C.: Cato Institute.

————. 2001. Economic growth and the state of humanity. *PERC Policy Series* PS-21 (April). Bozeman, Mont.: PERC.

Grossman, Gene M., and Alan B. Krueger. 1991. *Environmental impact of a North American free trade agreement.* Working Paper 3914. Cambridge, Mass.: National Bureau of Economic Research.

————. 1995. Economic growth and the environment. *Quarterly Journal of Economics* 110: 353–77.

Hettige, Hemamala, Robert E. B. Lucas, and David Wheeler. 1992. The toxic intensity of industrial production: Global patterns, trends, and trade policy. *American Economic Review* 82 (2): 478–81.

Hilton, F., G. Hank, and Arik Levinson. 1998. Factoring the environmental Kuznets curve: Evidence from automotive lead emissions. *Journal of Environmental Economics and Management* 35: 126–41.

Knack, Stephen, and Philip Keefer. 1995. Institutions and economic performance: Cross-country tests using alternative institutional measures. *Economics and Politics* 7 (3): 207–27.

Lomborg, Bjørn. 2001. *The skeptical environmentalist: Measuring the real state of the world.* New York: Cambridge University Press.

Norton, Seth W. 2002. Population growth, economic freedom, and the rule of law. *PERC Policy Series* PS-24 (February). Bozeman, Mont.: PERC.

Panayotou, Theodore. 1995. Environmental degradation at different stages of economic development. In *Beyond Rio: The environmental crisis and sustainable livelihoods in the third world,* ed. I. Ahmed and J. A. Doeleman. ILO Studies Series. New York: St. Martin's Press.

————. 1997. Demystifying the environmental Kuznets curve: Turning a black box into a policy tool. *Environment and Development Economics* 2: 465–84.

Qin, Xiang Dong. 1998. Economic development and environmental quality: A look at the environmental Kuznets curve. Dissertation. Clemson, S.C.: Clemson University.

Ridley, Matt. 1996. *The origins of virtue.* New York: Viking-Penguin Press.

————. 2002. Technology and the environment: The case for optimism. ATSE Focus 120, The Australian Academy of Technology, Sciences, and Engineering (January/February). Online: http://atse.org.au/publications/focus/focus-ridley.htm.

Schumpeter, Joseph. 1975 [1942]. *Capitalism, socialism and democracy.* New York: Harper.

Seldon, Thomas M., and Daqing Song. 1994. Environmental quality and development: Is there a Kuznets curve for air pollution emissions? *Journal of Environmental Economics and Management* 27: 147–62.

Shafik, Nemat. 1994. Economic development and environmental quality: An econometric analysis. *Oxford Economic Papers* 46: 757–77.

Shafik, Nemat, and Sushenjit Bandyopadhyay. 1992. Economic growth and environmental quality: Time series and cross section evidence. Working paper. Washington, D.C.: World Bank.

Simon, Julian L. 1981. *The ultimate resource.* Princeton, N.J.: Princeton University Press.

Stern, David I., and Michael S. Common. 2001. Is there an environmental Kuznets curve for sulfur? *Journal of Environmental Economics and Management* 41: 162–78.

Suri, Vivek, and Duane Chapman. 1998. Economic growth, trade, and energy: Implications for the environmental Kuznets curve. *Ecological Economics* 25 (May 2): 195–208.

Torras, Mariano, and James K. Boyce. 1998. Income, inequality, and pollution: A reassessment of the environmental Kuznets curve. *Ecological Economics* 25 (2): 147–60.

Wildavsky, Aaron. 1988. *Searching for safety.* New Brunswick, N.J.: Transaction Books.

World Bank. 1992. World development report 1992: Development and the environment. Washington, D.C.: World Bank.

World Resources Institute. 1990. *World Resources 1990–91.* New York: Oxford University Press.

Chapter 4

Globalization, Free Trade, and Environmental Quality

B. Delworth Gardner

GLOBALIZATION IS A WORD on many lips these days for both good and ill. In fact, seldom have opinions on any subject been so diverse and strongly held. Some see it as a panacea for solving most of the serious economic problems in the world, while others see it as a capitalist plot leading to oppression, exploitation, and injustice. Most observers, however, are between such extremes and see pros and cons. Recent books (for example, Friedman 2000, Stiglitz 2002, Lindsey 2002a, Blustein 2002, Bhagwati 2002, and Irwin 2002a) provide various interpretations of globalization's scope and merit. And Bjørn Lomborg's book (2001) makes a persuasive case that globalization is an important contributor to improving environmental quality almost everywhere in the world. This view is sharply at variance with that of some of the most vocal

B. Delworth Gardner is professor emeritus of economics at Brigham Young University; professor emeritus of agricultural economics at the University of California, Davis; and a 2002 PERC Julian Simon Fellow. Ryan Anderson, research assistant at PERC in Bozeman, Montana, and Tara Olson, research assistant at Brigham Young University, were helpful in literature search and checking references. Terry L. Anderson provided many useful suggestions in the final editing.

critics of globalization, many of whom argue that environmental degradation is the inevitable consequence of free trade.

So, what is globalization anyway? A minimal definition would
include: (1) liberalization of international trade in goods and services;
(2) relatively free movement of people across national borders, both for
work and for pleasure; (3) mobility of capital worldwide; and (4) free
flow of information among nations. Some scholars believe that globalization will continue its inexorable advance, whereas others think it may
have already peaked and begun to decline. The central focus of this
chapter is the relationship between globalization and environmental
quality. Other issues discussed are: (1) how per-capita income is
affected by trade liberalization; (2) how increases in income affect
environmental quality; and (3) what the future prospects are for globalization and free trade in view of the critiques made against them and
recent developments that are protectionist, such as the steel tariffs and
the 2002 farm bill.

The Income Gains from Trade

Near unanimity now exists among economists that free trade increases
aggregate income and wealth. As long as it is negotiated without coer-
cion, trade is a positive-sum activity because all parties making
exchanges expect to benefit. In the late eighteenth century, Adam Smith
demonstrated how gains from trade among countries could enhance
wealth through specialization of labor and an extension of the size of
the market. In 1817, David Ricardo published his famous principle of
comparative advantage, which postulated that beneficial trade occurs
as long as differences exist in the ratios of costs of production (and
relative prices) of various goods in the trading countries.[1]

What might cause international differences in the pretrade cost
ratios of various goods? The Heckscher-Ohlin theorem postulates that
the most important reason is the difference among countries in factor
endowments (Takayama 1972, 70). A country will export goods that

more intensively utilize resources that are relatively more abundant and therefore cheaper. If a country has a relative abundance of resources that are closely associated with environmental quality (for example, forests, farmland, fresh water), free trade will lead to more intensive uses of those resources and, hence, may lead to a decline in environmental quality.

For classical liberals, an economic system that utilizes private property, free exchange, and unregulated market prices stands at the core of "liberty" and liberty could well be even more highly valued than income gains from trade. As *The Economist* (2001, 14) explains: "McDonald's does not march people into its outlets at the point of a gun. Nike does not require people to wear its trainers on pain of imprisonment. If people buy those things, it is because they choose to, not because globalization forces them to." Fortunately, as a general rule, liberty and income generation are not competitive but are complementary—as a consequence of liberty, society as a whole prospers, and it does this spontaneously, rather than by design of any person or government.

Let us now turn specifically to how much an economy might expect to benefit from trade liberalization. Sachs and Warner (1995) found that gross domestic product (GDP) in developing countries with open economies grew by 4.5 percent annually in the 1970s and 1980s, but that those with closed economies grew by only 0.7 percent annually. Frankel and Romer (1999) estimated that a 1 percent increase in the trade share of an economy increased per-capita income by about 0.8 percent—a relatively large impact from trade expansion. Another study (Harrison, Rutherford, and Tarr 1996) found that agreements to reduce trade barriers reached under the General Agreement on Tariffs and Trade (GATT) Uruguay Round in 1994 resulted "in an annual gain of $13 billion for the United States, about 0.2 percent of its GDP, and about $96 billion in gains for the world, roughly 0.4 percent of world GDP" (Irwin 2002a, 31). Yet another study (Brown, Deardorff, and Stern 2001) estimated that "if a new trade round reduced the world's tariffs on agricultural and industrial goods and barriers on services trade by one-third, the welfare gain for the United States would be $177 billion, or 1.95 percent of GDP. . . . The gain for the world would amount to $613 billion, or about 2 percent of world GDP" (Irwin 2002a, 31).

Evaluating the impact of the North American Free Trade Agreement (NAFTA), Irwin (2002a, 32) reports the findings of Roland-Holst, Reinhardt, and Schiells (1992) that moving from the assumption of constant returns to scale to the assumption, permitted by trade, of increasing returns to scale "boosted the calculated U.S. welfare gains from 1.67 percent to 2.55 percent of its GDP, Canadian gains ranged from 4.87 percent to 6.75 percent of its GDP, while the gains for Mexico were from 2.28 percent to 3.29 percent of its GDP."

Perhaps the most persuasive evidence of the beneficial effects of trade liberalization is the economic performance of those developing countries that have greatly expanded trade over the past few decades (the so-called Asian tigers: Taiwan, Singapore, Hong Kong, and South Korea) compared with those that have chosen to discourage trade through "import substitution" policies (much of Latin America and most of Africa). The income growth rates of the former group have been spectacular, whereas none of the latter group has had steady economic growth. Import substitution failed as an economic doctrine because trade protection policies produced vast distortions in relative prices and increased production costs (Perkins et al. 2001, 38).

The tiny island of Taiwan provides a shining example of what can occur when a country follows a liberal trade policy. Now the world's fifth-largest trading nation and eighteenth-largest economy, in less than forty years Taiwan's real per-capita income has risen from about $200 to over $13,000. Taiwan's huge neighbor, the People's Republic of China, offers another example. Since opening its economy to international trade and investment in the 1970s, China has grown at annual rates nearing or exceeding double digits (Perkins et al. 2001, 76–78).

The societal economic benefits from free trade extend beyond income gains. As Irwin (2002a, 34–36) points out:

> To the extent that economists focus only on trade's effects on production or income, they understate the gains from trade. . . . By overlooking effects on variety, the standard calculations of gains from trade clearly understate the true advantages of international commerce. . . . Trade improves economic performance not only by allocating a country's resources to their most efficient use, but by making those resources more productive in what they are doing. . . . International trade contributes to productivity growth in at least two ways: It serves as a conduit for the transfer of foreign technologies that enhance productivity, and it increases competition in a way that stimulates industries to become more efficient and improve their productivity, often by forcing less productive firms out of business and allowing more productive firms to expand.

As Irwin suggests, an important benefit from international trade is the importation of technological advance from trading partners. "Between a quarter and a half of growth in U.S. total factor productivity may be attributed to new technology embodied in capital equipment" (Irwin 2002a, 36). Eaton and Kortum (2001) found that "about a quarter of the differences in productivity across countries is due to differences in the prices of capital equipment . . . countries more open to trade gain more from foreign research and development expenditures" (Irwin 2002a, 36–37). Another study (Keller, 2000) corroborated this conclusion by finding that a country's total factor productivity depends not only on its own research and development (R&D), but also on how much R&D is conducted in the countries with which it trades. Developing countries that conduct little R&D themselves benefit from that done elsewhere because trade makes the acquisition of new technology less costly (Irwin 2002a, 37).

This brief review of empirical studies provides support for the theory that trade liberalization has a significant positive impact on the creation of income and wealth, as well as a number of other beneficial effects.

A current concern is that trends toward the increasing globalization and freer trade of recent years may not continue in light of recent events, such as the tragedy of September 11, 2001, and the subsequent war on terrorism, the economic meltdown in Argentina and other countries, the slowdown in the economic growth of most developed countries, the performance failure of prominent American business and accounting firms, and the recent turn toward protectionism in the United States and the retaliation of other countries that has already begun. In 2001, the rate of growth in world trade slowed sharply, to 2 percent from a growth rate of 12 percent in 2000 (*Wall Street Journal* 2002a). Much could be said about each of the reasons for the slowdown, but a few additional remarks will have to suffice.

The terrorist disaster of September 11, 2001, and related events have produced significant changes in the trade environment. People and goods moving among nations are monitored much more closely and trade is much more costly (*The Economist* 2002b, 13). The turn toward protectionism by the Bush administration and the U.S. Congress is also a major setback for free trade. On March 5, 2002, the Bush administration announced a comprehensive plan to protect the steel industry by imposing 30 percent tariffs on the main products of most of the big integrated mills. Other steel products will face tariffs from 8 percent to 15 percent.

The European Union (EU) is leading a counteroffensive by "demanding compensation for the cost of the steel tariffs" (*The Economist* 2002a, 63). In a rare act of prudence, however, it put off any direct retaliation against the U.S. tariffs with tariffs of their own, although it may take such action later (*Wall Street Journal* 2002b, A14). The Japanese also are threatening retaliation. Especially disturbing to free traders is that all sides in the dispute insist that their actions are consistent with global trading rules and that they are erecting protectionist measures only in order to promote free trade.

It is true that the U.S. Congress has now given trade promotion authority (TPA, sometimes called "fast-track") to the president, a concession never given to President Clinton. It commits Congress to vote up or down (that is, without amendments) on trade agreements. But Brink Lindsey argues that the way the TPA fight was fought will make it more difficult to get trade liberalization. "The Bush administration made one concession after another to protectionist and pro-subsidy lobbies—imposing steep duties on steel and lumber; caving in to the textile industry; bringing pressure against opening markets to Caribbean, South American, and Pakistani goods; and, perhaps worst of all, acquiescing in egregiously profligate new farm subsidies" (Lindsey 2002b, A14). The TPA bill also instructs American trade negotiators to regard labor and environmental goals as principal negotiating objectives and protects the antidumping rules that have been used for protectionist purposes in the past (*The Economist* 2002c, 57). It remains to be seen, therefore, whether the Bush administration can be effective in pushing a trade-expansion agenda.

The two industries that have proved most resistant to trade liberalization—and yet are of critical importance to the developing countries—are agriculture and textiles. At the Uruguay round of the GATT, the developed countries agreed to limit agricultural export subsidies, but no real change has occurred. The 2003 Doha meeting of the World Trade Organization (WTO), the existence of which is another outcome of the Uruguay round, produced an agreement that agricultural export subsidies as well as general agricultural subsidies within the developed countries would be eliminated.

So what did the United States actually do in farm policy? The Farm Security and Rural Investment Act was passed by Congress and signed by President Bush on May 13, 2002. It increases farm subsidies to unprecedented levels and will likely undermine any hopes of liberalizing agricultural trade. It is ironic, in fact, that "it was the Americans who insisted on putting freer trade in agriculture at the heart of the Doha round" (*The Economist* 2002a, 66).

As to the effects on trade, perhaps even more important than the dollar amount of the subsidies is the way they are structured. The 1996 farm bill decoupled income-support payments for the basic crops (cotton, rice, wheat, feed grains) from the quantity produced. Hence, the payments themselves had little output-increasing effects. The new farm bill, however, allows the base acreage and base yields that determine the amounts of government payments to each farm to be updated to 2001. The effect will be to provide incentives to increase output, which will augment the need for American farmers to increase exports. Since the United States is the world's largest agricultural exporter (roughly half of corn, wheat, cotton, and rice is exported), the impact on world prices will probably be significant. As a consequence, incomes of farmers in countries that depend on agricultural exports could be catastrophically reduced (Thurow and Kilman 2002). Given the American farm bill, the EU, which was reluctant to place agriculture on the negotiating table at Doha, will likely put off any reduction in their own farm subsidies (*The Economist* 2002a, 63–66).

The Doha agreement also addresses textiles—it calls for the quota system on textiles to be phased out by 2005, which would benefit developing countries. Given the political pressure for protection, however, the prospects for significant and permanent change in textiles may be just as dismal as for agricultural reform. In sum, the next decade, and perhaps beyond, may not be a happy time for free traders.

Trade and the Environment

The nexus between international trade and environmental quality is more complex than appears at first blush. Three connections will be explored in this section: (1) increases in incomes and demand for environmental quality; (2) direct trading in environmental goods; and (3) indirect effects of trade on environmental regulation and technical change.

Income and Environmental Quality

If free trade unambiguously increases average per-capita income as argued earlier, what can be said about the relationship between the level and growth of income and environmental quality?

A major contribution to what is known about trade and the environment is Bjørn Lomborg's outstanding book *The Skeptical Environmentalist* (2001).[2] Lomborg's first chapter, "Things Are Getting Better," is a comprehensive survey of the current state of the world's environment. Lomborg uses the same indicators and data sources as those utilized by prominent "green" organizations whose allegations include an increasing population overrunning the capacity of the world to feed itself; falling levels of human health; shrinking forests; eroding soils; declining water quality; falling groundwater tables; disappearing wetlands; collapsing fisheries; deteriorating rangelands; rising world temperatures; dying corral reefs; and disappearing plant and animal species. In a *tour de force*, Lomborg demonstrates that fears of these deteriorating conditions are unfounded—instead of the environment getting worse, it is actually improving in nearly all respects.

Lomborg (2001, 29) also indicates why this improvement is occurring. Trade and less costly transport effectively act to reduce risks and make local areas less vulnerable to natural resource exhaustion and depletion. This is a tremendously important insight. In a trading economy, production does not necessarily have to take place at the physical location of demand, but where it is most efficient. An implication is that as resource scarcity occurs and prices and costs rise in a trading world, production will shift to other locations with less scarcity and lower prices and costs. The effect is that each country can almost indefinitely postpone running into a wall imposed by resource scarcity, and all of the trading economies will benefit.

Lomborg makes another salient point: "We have grown to believe that we are faced with an inescapable choice between higher economic welfare and a greener environment. But, surprisingly . . . environmental development often stems from economic development—only when we get sufficiently rich can we afford the relative luxury of caring about the environment" (Lomborg 2001, 32–33).

Direct Trade in Environmental Goods

Another way that international trade and the environment are related is through direct trading in environmental goods, such as debt-for-nature swaps and pollution-emission rights, both of which have become prominent in the past two decades. Gains from trade may be large because of differences among countries in their endowments of nature and in their preferences for environmental goods.

A debt-for-nature swap typically involves three or more parties: an international conservation organization (such as the Nature Conservancy or the WWF), a conservation organization from the country where the conservation work is to be done (host country), and one or more government agencies in the host country. The international conservation organization desires to maintain or improve the environment in the host country and is willing to pay because its members place high value on environmental amenities. The host-country conservation organization has the interest and presumed competence needed to manage a conservation project, and the host-country governmental organizations facilitate the transfer of the debt, for a price, and will generally disburse the funds (Deacon and Murphy 1993, 1997).

The process ordinarily begins when the debtor country's central bank agrees to sell some of its external debt, usually because the country has a problem generating foreign exchange and does not have the hard currency to pay its foreign debts. The international environmental organization can often acquire the debt at a significant discount, especially if it is willing to take the proceeds in the currency of the host country— no problem, since the host country is where the expenditures for environmental improvement will occur.

A swap normally requires that the host country place domestic currency bonds in an environmental trust fund held in the country's central bank where the funds will be at the disposal of the international conservation organization and disbursed to the host-country conservation organization. Deacon and Murphy (1993) analyzed some of the contracts covering these swaps and identified the transaction costs inherent in them. Costs tend to be large for several reasons: coping with conventional free-rider problems, specifying the desired environmental goods and services, monitoring the provider's conservation input and its shirking, and facing host-country public resentment over the threat of lost national sovereignty imposed by the agreements (Deacon and Murphy 1993, 69).

The lack of enforceability of these contracts is a severe impediment to originating these swaps and explains why thus far they have been concentrated in a small number of developing countries. Deacon and Murphy (1997) inquire if there are attributes of countries that predispose them to become involved in swaps with the developed world, and they find, *a priori*, that these swaps are more likely in countries where threats to species and other environmental resources are most acute and in those that have heavy debt burdens. Also, swaps are expected to be more prevalent in countries with a stable rule of law, which is conducive to honoring contracts. Empirical data confirm the validity of these expectations (13).

Direct trading for the right to emit pollutants among countries also has potential for reducing the costs of international agreements to control pollution. The Kyoto Protocol, for example, specifies emission targets for each participant developed country (the developing countries were exempted from the agreement). The protocol also establishes, however, the possibility of trading rights for carbon dioxide emissions that might affect the atmosphere of all countries. Countries would be given allowances to emit carbon dioxide, but then could buy and sell these rights at a negotiated price. All trading countries could be made better off in trading pollution rights to those countries in which the costs of reducing emissions are highest. Lomborg (2001) cites studies (for example, Nordhaus and Boyer 1999) showing that the cost of the Kyoto Protocol would be $346 billion a year with no trades in emission rights, whereas with trade permitted among the rich countries the cost drops to $161 billion annually. If trade were global among all countries, the aggregate cost would be even lower, at $75 billion. Since these potential gains are so large, trading markets would surely arise and institutions would surely be fashioned to accommodate them. The United States argued strongly for this trading strategy but has withdrawn from the protocol, so perhaps the most powerful advocate for emissions trading within the protocol is now gone (Lomborg 2001, 303).

Environmental Regulation and Technical Change

A seminal paper by Antweiler, Copeland, and Taylor (2001) provides convincing theoretical and empirical evidence that international trade is good for the environment. They postulate that trade affects environmental quality through three channels: (1) the location of production; (2) the scale of production; and (3) the techniques of production. Their econometric model estimates the independent effects of each of these channels on variation in the concentrations of sulfur dioxide in the air among the countries sampled. Changes in the location of production attributable to international trade are found to be empirically trivial. Freer trade results in an increase in the scale of production, and this effect has a modest negative impact on environmental quality (more output is associated with a little more pollution). A 1 percent increase in the scale of production raises pollution concentrations by 0.25 to 0.5 percent for an average country in the sample. It is the increase in income produced by trade liberalization that is the dominating force, driving concentrations of pollutants down by a significant amount (1.25 to 1.5 percent) via the technique effect (Antweiler, Copeland, and Taylor 2001, 877–78). The critical explanatory factor is that wealthier countries value environmental amenities more highly and enhance their production by employing environmentally friendly technologies.

The findings of this study are in sharp contrast to what some of the most vocal opponents of globalization and free trade believe, which is that if companies are to be internationally competitive as free trade requires, governments have no choice but to dismantle health, safety, and environmental regulations. In the language of the day, international competition induces a "regulatory race to the bottom."

On a purely theoretical level, the work of Heckscher (1949) and Ohlin (1933) implies that trade might induce countries rich in natural resources (and associated environmental amenities) to utilize these resources more intensively and hence reduce environmental quality. On the other hand, this theory also predicts that polluting, capital-intensive manufacturing will tend to locate in the richer developed countries, where capital is relatively cheap. Hence, on the basis of theory alone the net environmental effects are ambiguous, so the question must be settled by empirical evidence.

Jagdish Bhagwati (2002) argues that although the race-to-the-bottom argument may be theoretically valid, it fails on empirical grounds. Little evidence exists that governments actually play the competitive game by offering to cut standards or that multinational corporations are seduced by such concessions (58–59).

Indeed, most recent trade agreements affirm the right of each country to choose its own level of environmental protection. The North American Free Trade Agreement (NAFTA), for example, specifically provides that no member country should relax its health, safety, and environmental standards for the purpose of attracting or retaining investment in its territory. Moreover, arbitration tribunals are established specifically to referee protests and conflict, including those in the environmental arena (Globerman 1993, 28).

What about the possibility that national governments competing for trade will be less inclined to pass and enforce environmental standards, given the industrial dislocations and short-term unemployment that are alleged to arise from trade liberalization? Globerman (1993, 38) argues that empirical evidence does not support this contention either. Canadian and American protective tariffs have been reduced over time, yet there has been neither diminution of environmental standards nor enforcement of them. In the EU, pressure from those countries enforcing the rules and adopting their own tough antipollution laws is apparently bringing about compliance by all members. The bottom line is that each country must decide for itself what the optimal combination of trade and environmental policies suits it best because of differences in preferences, income, and the assimilative capacities of natural resources.

Lomborg cites a 1972 World Bank study that investigated whether there is a general tendency for economic growth to lead to lower environmental quality initially, but then later for growth to push in the opposite direction. The study found that in the first phases of growth, countries tend to pollute more, after which their pollution levels fall. Lomborg argues that pollution has fallen for all nations at all levels of wealth and believes that "this is due to continuing technological development, which makes it possible to produce the same amount of goods while imposing less of a burden on the environment. Developing countries can buy progressively cheaper, cleaner technology from the West" (2001, 176).

In specific reference to NAFTA, Bruce Yandle (1993, 8) observes:

[T]he Office of the U.S. Trade Representative developed a "hit list" of industries vulnerable to the intertwined forces of reduced tariffs and high-cost pollution control. . . . After examining 445 U.S. industries, the analysts found eleven vulnerable to the effects of environmental rules, reduced tariffs, and relaxed investment restrictions. The "hit list" industries are specialty steel, petroleum refining, five categories of chemicals, including medicinal compounds, iron foundries, blast furnaces, and steel mills, explosives, and mineral wool. Probing deeper, the commission's report notes that ten of the eleven industries have high capital intensity, thus reducing the likelihood that plants will relocate to take advantage of lower environmental costs in Mexico. . . . Finally, environmental quality may improve because new plants tend to use the latest technology and equipment, which reduce inefficiencies and pollution.

The main implication of the trade commission's study is that without searching and detailed analysis, industry-by-industry, environmental problems alleged to be the consequence of trade liberalization will likely be grossly exaggerated.

Other studies turn the question around—how do environmental regulations affect trade flows? Antweiler, Copeland, and Taylor (2001, 879) suggest that

> [a] common result from these studies is that measures of environmental stringency have little effect on trade flows. This result immediately casts doubt on the pollution-haven hypothesis, which holds that trade in dirty goods primarily responds to cross-country differences in regulations. . . . We too find little support for the pollution-haven hypothesis. We do not infer from this, however, that the cost of regulations does not matter to trade flows; instead, we suggest it is because other offsetting factors more than compensate for the costs of tight regulation in developed countries.

A good example of trade effects on the environment can be found in agricultural commerce. Liberalization in trading agricultural commodities would probably shift production away from the EU and Japan where it is expensive and chemical-intensive, to developing countries, which use far less pesticide and fertilizer that do environmental damage. Further, the reduction of agricultural subsidies that might result from free-trade agreements would reduce the incentive to cultivate marginal lands in developed countries and thereby reduce soil erosion and increase wildlife habitat (Patterson 1993, 62; Gardner 1995).

A final point on the relationships between technical change and the environment is that rapid technological change makes predictions about future long-term environmental change extremely hazardous. For example, a model developed by Chakravorty, Roumasset, and Tse (1997) simulates the effects on the world's biosphere of carbon-dioxide emissions from the burning of carbon fuels. These scholars argue that "popular predictions of the probable extent of global warming are based on models that do not generally account for price-induced energy conservation, including endogenous substitution between alternative energy sources, cost-saving improvements in extraction technology, and the rapidly declining cost of solar-powered electricity generation" (p. 1200). Using data on extraction costs, estimated reserves, and energy demand for the world economy, Chakravorty, Roumasset, and Tse find that if historical rates of cost reduction in the production of solar energy are maintained, more than 90 percent of the world's coal reserves will never be used as the world shifts from coal, oil, and natural gas to solar energy. As this occurs, global temperatures will rise by only about 1.5 to 2.0 degrees centigrade by the middle of the twenty-first century, then will decline steadily to pre-industrial levels. Carbon emissions will continue to increase for the next three decades followed by a sharp drop (1201–1203). These findings demonstrate that serious forecasting mistakes will be made unless the effects of technological change are included in analyses of environmental problems.

Despite the manifest and substantial beneficial effects of globalization and trade on the environment as discussed, numerous critics have raised objections, some of them specifically on the grounds that freer trade will result in the degradation of the environment. Even those who oppose globalization for other than environmental reasons are unwittingly and indirectly harming the environment. For this reason, these critics and their contentions will be discussed next.

Critics of Globalization and Free Trade

The main classes of opponents to globalization are those in protected domestic industries (including their labor unions and political supporters), many environmental groups, politically radical protestors who despise capitalism, a few leaders of developing countries who view globalization as a threat to their political and economic autonomy, and some academics and intellectuals who are primarily critics of the international institutions of globalization, especially the International Monetary Fund (IMF) and the World Trade Organization (WTO).

Trade and the Distribution of Income

The trade unions in protected domestic industries are among the staunchest opponents of trade liberalization. They argue that free trade will worsen the relative economic position of working people and increase inequality in the distribution of income. Are they correct?

The Stolper-Samuelson (1941) factor-price-equalization theorem establishes a theoretical link between trade and the distribution of income. The theorem postulates that the relative and absolute prices of the factors of production (for example, labor, capital, land) eventually will be equalized between trading countries. The most interesting implication of the theorem is that even with complete absence of movement of the factors of production among countries, the competitive forces of trade in goods will move factor prices toward equality. Hence, if labor is poorly paid in developing countries (relative to its productivity) compared with wages in rich countries, trade can be expected to reduce the disparity of wages between countries. Equivalently, relatively abundant and cheap factors in an economy will gain from trade liberalization and relatively costly factors will lose. For example, the United States has a relative abundance of land and capital as reflected in their relative prices and a relative scarcity of labor compared with most other countries. The United States, therefore, exports land- and capital-intensive goods and imports labor-intensive goods. Hence, a tariff on labor-intensive goods will increase the relative price of these goods and increase the real wages of workers in the United States who produce them. The tariff shifts factors of production from the export-goods industry to the import-competing-goods industry. *Ceteris paribus*, the tariff can be expected to increase wages and decrease land rents—implying that labor unions in the United States will favor trade protection while farmers and land-owners will be free traders.

The real world, however, is more complex than is implied in this simple explication of the theory. For one thing, labor is not homogeneous, especially in modern developed countries. Some labor embodies large amounts of human and scientific capital (science-intensive labor) while other labor embodies very little (unskilled labor). If the United States has an abundance of science-intensive labor relative to other countries, free trade will induce exportation of goods that utilize science-intensive labor. A tariff on goods that use unskilled labor will increase unskilled wages relative to science-intensive wages. Because poor people in the United States tend to be relatively unskilled, protection of those industries that utilize unskilled labor will tend to reduce inequality in the distribution of income.

What do empirical studies show about how the gains from trade are distributed between and within trading countries? Does free trade harm the poor while benefiting the rich in both developing and developed countries, as is alleged by many critics of globalization?

Rodrik (1997) finds that because capital is more mobile across countries than is labor, the competitive force of globalization leads to lower taxes on capital and higher taxes on labor. Because capital is owned disproportionately by the wealthy, lower taxes on capital would increase income disparity. Rodrik (1998) also argues that the downward leveling of capital taxes across countries may raise the tax burden on labor to politically unacceptable levels or else will compromise social and worker protection programs that in his view have allowed countries gradually to lower trade barriers over the postwar period (Obstelfd 1998, 20). But on the other hand, lower taxes on capital will encourage saving and investing and thus lead to higher levels of labor productivity, economic growth, and higher living standards across the board.

Models of interindustry trade among rich countries have shown that the exploitation of scale economies made possible by trade generally increases the demand for skilled labor and its relative reward compared with unskilled labor (Bhagwati 2002, 83). Larger markets made possible by trade increase returns from innovation and investments in R&D as well as from human capital, and in this regard, the results of trade are similar to those of technological advance.

A study by Cline cited without reference in *The Economist* (2001) estimates that technological change is five times more powerful in widening short-term inequality in America than globalization. Cline also found that both trade and technological advances are overwhelmed in importance by the main force operating in the opposite direction to reduce income inequality: namely, investment in human capital through education and training (*The Economist* 2001, 9).

The Stolper-Samuelson theorem also implies that globalization may produce displacement of some workers in rich countries, leaving them worse off, but Bhagwati (2002, 89) believes that the evidence for this in the United States is weak. One of the reasons is that large trade deficits in the current account in the 1980s, when pressure on real wages was significant, were accompanied by large surpluses in the capital account. This inflow of direct foreign investment increased either jobs or wages or both. For these and other reasons, Bhagwati argues that the alarm of the unions over the adverse effects of free trade on the real wages of workers in rich countries is far from persuasive.

Another important reason that the negative effects of trade on employment may be exaggerated is that nontraded services have become an increasingly higher proportion of aggregate production and employment. Only about 17 percent of American workers, those employed in agriculture, mining, and manufacturing, are now directly exposed to international competition, as opposed to 40 percent in 1960 (Irwin 2002a, 11). Because of free electronic information provided by the Internet revolution, however, this trend may not last. Micklethwait and Wooldridge (2002) show that at least part of the service industry (accounting, marketing, design, customer service, credit evaluation) is shifting to low-wage developing countries such as India, the Philippines, and Eastern Europe. Well-schooled and trained workers are benefiting in an unprecedented way, and so are consumers of these services across the world as costs and prices fall and real incomes rise.

What happens to jobs and wages in poor countries as their economies are liberalized? Here the critics of globalization clearly have it wrong. In theory, free trade will increase the demand for poor-country labor, pushing up wages, and competition for labor will benefit even those workers who are not employed in trade-related jobs. Openness to foreign trade and investment encourages capital flows to poor economies, in which the marginal productivity of capital tends to be higher, and this infusion of capital drives the marginal productivity of labor higher. Capital tends to be especially productive if it is provided by multinational corporations because the funds are usually packaged with imported skills and technology. There is little doubt that a major agent of globalization in the world is the multinational company—therefore, a favorite target of the political left. Multinational corporations account for most foreign direct investment as well as a rising share of foreign trade in the developing countries—maybe as much as two-thirds of manufacturing (Amsden 2002, 13).

A World Bank report issued in December 2001 finds, unsurprisingly, that trade and globalization have benefited some poor countries more than others. Globalization was measured as a rise in the ratio of trade to national income. The more-globalized poor countries grew at an average annual rate of 5 percent in the 1990s, whereas less-globalized poor countries shrank by 1 percent over the decade (World Bank Group 2001a). By comparison, rich countries grew at the rate of 2 percent.

Lomborg (2001, 74) shows that if per-capita income comparisons among nations are calculated in terms of the purchasing power of various currencies, the developing world has been catching up with the developed world since the 1950s. Lomborg sees no reasons why these trends will not continue throughout the next century. So much for the allegation frequently heard from critics of globalization that trade increases incomes in rich countries at the expense of incomes in poor countries.

Of course, many scholars believe that the distribution of income may be a poor proxy for the distribution of human well-being, even if reckoned in terms of purchasing power parity. Over the past century, advances in other indicators of well-being, such as increased mortality and reduced morbidity, have been captured by developing as well as developed countries. Diseases that have burdened mankind for centuries, especially in developing countries—plague, cholera, polio, small pox, tuberculosis, and malaria—have been controlled, if not eliminated, almost everywhere. The increasing prevalence of HIV infection and AIDS is a notable exception. Improved sanitation and water quality have reduced digestive tract diseases, and the availability and lower cost of drugs, from aspirin to quinine to antibiotics, have made life better across the globe. There can be little doubt that these improvements in human health and life longevity are at least partially attributable to globalization and trade (see chapter 2 in this volume).

What about the allegations frequently advanced by labor unions and the political left in developed countries that workers in developing countries lack the rights, legal protections, and union representation enjoyed by workers in rich countries and that labor is supposedly kept in poverty by being forced to work in sweatshops and that only capitalist owners benefit?

Bhagwati finds unpersuasive "the frequent complaint in some poor countries that free trade accentuates poverty. . . . The facts show that a shift out of autarky into closer integration into the world economy is producing better, not worse, results for poverty reduction" (2002, 89–90). Indeed, a recent study by the World Bank Group confirms this view by suggesting that trade liberalization of the kind contemplated by the Doha agreement would lift an extra 300 million people out of poverty by 2015 (2001b).

The most compelling evidence, however, is provided by the record of many developing countries in reducing poverty through trade liberalization. Those that have achieved sustained and rapid growth, such as those in East Asia, have made remarkable progress in poverty reduction. On the other hand, countries where widespread poverty persists are those in which growth is weakest, capitalism is least developed, and trade is practically nonexistent, as in sub-Saharan Africa, Myanmar, and North Korea. Improved property rights in land can also make a significant difference in alleviating poverty. As Hernando de Soto (2000) has shown in his remarkable book, *The Mystery of Capital*, it is the poor who suffer most from obstacles to small-scale enterprise and insecure titles to land.

Politically Radical Protestors of Capitalism

Among the most vociferous protesters at meetings of the IMF, the World Bank, and the WTO is a group of mostly young people of the political left who hate markets and capitalism. Bhagwati (2002, 5–8) asks why free trade has become the target of what seems to be a growing anticapitalist and antiglobalization movement among the young. He argues that two factors are primarily responsible. First, capitalism is perceived to be a source of injustice rather than as providing economic opportunity for the majority. And second, in their colleges and universities many young Americans have been taught the deconstructionist philosophy of Jacques Derrida, which propounds a political wasteland where belief and action yield to cynicism and anarchism and which feeds anti-intellectual attitudes.

Greg Rushford (2002) provides an illustration of the activities of these haters of globalization. "Fair-trade" coffee sells at premium prices at retail outlets and purports to have been produced by small-scale growers in Guatemala. These farmers are alleged to be pitted against a large coffee plantation that exploits its workers. Fair-trade coffee is represented in the United States by Global Exchange, a San Francisco–based group that targets big names in the coffee industry, including Starbucks and Procter & Gamble, and demands that they carry fair-trade coffee. Members of Global Exchange were active protesters at the WTO meetings at Seattle, Doha, Genoa, and New York. Rushford went to Guatemala to investigate the allegations of labor exploitation brought by Global Exchange and found that the plantation pays its workers about twice the existing minimum wage and, in addition, provides social benefits that are not available to coffee laborers who work off the plantation. Rushford concludes that the fair-trade coffee project of Global Exchange is a cleverly disguised effort to condemn capitalism.

I attended a rally at Dolores Park in San Francisco on April 20, 2002. The rally was widely advertised as a citizen protest against globalization and free trade. Most of the attendees were young (between ages 18 and 30), and it was apparent to me that they were serious about what they were doing. A series of speeches were virulent tirades aimed at capitalism, globalization, Israel and Prime Minister Ariel Sharon, President George W. Bush (mostly for the war on terrorism), free trade, the WTO, and the IMF. Hundreds of placards and banners held by the protesters contained the same invective as the speeches. It was obvious to me that the demonstrators would have joined the protesters at the WTO-IMF meetings if they could have, and perhaps many of them did.

Columbia University professor Joseph Stiglitz, fresh from appointments as chairman of President Clinton's Council of Economic Advisers and chief economist at the World Bank, writes: "It is the trade unionists, students, environmentalists—ordinary citizens—marching in the streets of Prague, Seattle, Washington, and Genoa who have put the need for reform [of the IMF and the WTO] on the agenda of the developed world" (2002, 9). Although the protesters at these meetings were undoubtedly a somewhat heterogeneous group as Stiglitz suggests, in my view it is hardly accurate to portray them as ordinary citizens in the sense that their views would represent those of most ordinary Americans.

Of the leaders of developing countries who are resisting globalization, perhaps the most prominent is Dr. Mahathir Mohamad, president of Malaysia. At the 2001 Shanghai meeting of the Asian Pacific Economic Cooperation, Mahathir opined that opening economies to free capital movement gives too much power to Western governments and investors who want to control, if not impoverish, poor nations. This view stands in stark contrast to the official communiqué of that conference, which states that economic globalization is really the only hope for ridding the world of poverty.

Of course, it is clearly evident that many less developed countries have benefited from global integration while many others have not. A recent study by the World Bank shows that 24 countries, home to more than three billion people, including China, Brazil, India, and the Philippines, have increased their trade-to-GDP ratios over the past 20 years, and their GDP growth rates have exceeded 5 percent annually during the 1990s. Other countries, however, with another two billion people, including most of sub-Saharan Africa as well as some countries in Asia and the Middle East, have become less rather than more globalized, and their growth rates are very low or even negative (World Bank Group 2001b). These facts support the inference that developing countries that do not open up their economies risk being left further and further behind.

Critics of the IMF and the WTO

Even among economists, the performance of the WTO and the IMF is controversial. Wide agreement exists as to the benefits of international capital mobility: Markets channel world saving to its most productive uses, irrespective of location; residents of different countries are allowed to pool various risks, hence achieving more effective insurance than purely domestic arrangements would produce; countries suffering economic downturns, a financial crisis due to depletion of foreign exchange, or natural disasters can borrow from abroad; and developing countries with inadequate capital or savings can borrow to finance investment, thereby promoting economic growth (Obstfeld 1998, 10).

But, it is argued, a significant downside to rapid capital movements has surfaced in the financial crises in Mexico, Russia, East Asia, Brazil, Argentina and, recently, Uruguay. Long-term foreign direct investments are not the problem because they are illiquid and cannot flee a country on short notice. Short-term "hot money," however, which chases international differences in interest rates, can be withdrawn quickly, often producing large changes in foreign exchange reserves, especially if the loans are denominated in hard foreign currencies (for example, dollars) and the exchange rate is pegged in order to reduce the risk of currency fluctuations. Countries in this situation are vulnerable to speculative attacks on their currency and may face the threat of contagion from financial crises elsewhere (Rodrick 1997, 5).

The critics of globalization (and of the WTO and the IMF) from the political left argue that international financial and trade liberalization itself contributes to financial crises. Liberalization imposes crippling debts on poor countries, exposes them to fluctuations of the global business cycle, delivers windfall profits to domestic and foreign speculators, and weakens rules that protect consumers and workers from abuse (*The Economist* 2001, 21).

Professor Stiglitz is an unabashed critic of the organizations of globalization, especially the IMF. He believes that the rich countries are rigging the globalization agenda so as to benefit themselves (2002, 7). In fact, Stiglitz argues that the IMF has not fulfilled the lofty objective promised by its founding, to help developing countries grow by using expansionary macroeconomic policies, such as increasing government expenditures and lowering interest rates. Instead, today the IMF typically provides loans only if recipient countries do the exact opposite, such as cutting deficits, raising taxes, and increasing interest rates—all of which lead to a contraction of the economy (12–13). Many economists agree with Stiglitz that IMF prescriptions for economies in financial crises are often inappropriate as remedies for the economic downturns that inevitably accompany these crises.

That borrowing countries must share the blame, however, is seldom admitted by the left. Governments that channel foreign borrowings into large budget deficits and consumption rather than into sound investment inevitably have problems generating resources to repay loans.

Some countries have openly encouraged foreign borrowing in excessive amounts, knowing that international agencies will bail them out if repayment trouble arises (*The Economist* 2001, 22).

Criticism of the international financial institutions by the political right is quite different and focuses on the moral-hazard problem. The IMF sees its role primarily as protecting rich-country lenders against loan defaults by borrowing countries. Because rich-country bond-holders have been bailed out by the IMF time and again when crises occurred, excessively risky uses of funds have been encouraged. Hence, IMF lending creates perverse incentives for international lenders as well as international borrowers.

The ubiquity and severity of these moral-hazard problems have prompted some free-market economists to recommended abolishing the IMF entirely. They argue that "without an IMF, if a country runs out of hard currency, its foreign creditors would be forced to accept whatever they could get in negotiations or lawsuits. . . . [E]veryone would take care to avoid a crisis, knowing how disastrous the consequences would be. Government officials would run more prudent economic policies, and international money managers would be more vigilant about where its money goes" (Blustein 2002, 379). In short, proper incentives would be put in place to produce more responsible and efficient financial decisions.

The international financial crises of the past two decades prompted the United States Congress to appoint a blue-ribbon commission to investigate whether the IMF should be reorganized. Chaired by Professor Allan Meltzer of Carnegie Mellon University, the commission recommended fundamental changes in the way the organization operates. IMF loans would go only to countries that got a "seal of approval" in advance from the IMF by meeting various criteria of sound economic policy, including adherence to standards that ensure that banks maintain sufficient capital. Hence, the IMF would not need to impose policy conditions when it made loans. These reforms in IMF policies seem responsive to the criticisms from both political left and right. But Blustein sees a potential problem with the recommendation: "Suppose the IMF had to drop a country from the list of prequalifiers; imagine how fast a crisis would erupt in that country" (2002, 380–81).

The WTO has been criticized, especially by environmentalist critics, on the grounds that it is an international bureaucracy that is unanswerable to any democratic process. These antidemocratic powers supposedly inhere in the organization's dispute-resolution procedures, which were strengthened in the Uruguay round of the GATT. Irwin (2002a), however, disputes this negative conclusion. He argues that the power to make trade policy and to write the governing rules really resides with the member governments, not with the WTO. The WTO provides only a forum for consultations and negotiations and has no power to force countries to obey the agreements or to comply with its rulings (Irwin 2002a, 186).

An apt illustration is provided by the WTO rules on environmental quality (World Trade Organization 1999, 455). Irwin (2002a, 191–92) refers to a General Accounting Office study that found:

> WTO rulings to date against U.S. environmental measures have not weakened U.S. environmental protections. . . . And these few environmental cases have mainly focused on whether the regulation in question has been implemented in a nondiscriminatory way, not whether that regulation is justifiable. . . . The most relevant provision of the GATT is Article 20, entitled "General Exceptions." Subject to the requirement that such measures are not applied in a manner which would constitute a means of arbitrary or unjustifiable discrimination between countries where the same conditions prevail, or a disguised restriction on international trade, nothing in the Agreement shall be construed to prevent the adoption or enforcement by any contracting party of measures . . . (b) necessary to protect human, animal, or plant life or health . . . [or] (g) relating to the conservation of exhaustible natural resources if such measures are made effective in conjunction with restrictions on domestic production or consumption.

There is also little empirical support for the contention that national policies to protect the environment are irreparably threatened by WTO rules. The principal strength of the WTO trading system, in fact, is that all countries, including small ones, can receive fair treatment under the rule of law. "The alternative is that more powerful countries simply dictate outcomes to others" (Irwin 2002b, 73).

Irwin also vigorously disputes the allegations of some environmentalists that WTO rules militate against environmental quality. He argues that although there may be tensions between trade policy and environmental objectives, the world trade rules *per se* are not inherently anti-environment. Many WTO decisions reaffirm the rule that countries can maintain their own environmental regulations, so long as they are not discriminatory. And Irwin strongly holds the view that unilateral trade sanctions are a poor instrument for achieving environmental goals and that international agreements on standards are clearly preferable to trade embargoes (Irwin 2002b, 77).

Conclusions

Strong empirical evidence supports economic theory that free international trade creates growth in per-capita income and wealth as well as other societal benefits, such as individual liberty. The great spurts of modern economic growth occurring over the past 200 years, both in individual countries and in the world as a whole, have coincided closely with periods of liberalization of trade and commerce. Those developing countries that have made the most economic progress since World War II are those that have liberalized trade and promoted exports. Those that have turned inward and followed import-substitution policies are almost all economic basket cases. Political democratization, entrepreneurial development, rapid technological advance, free-flowing scientific information, and open capital markets are synergistic with each other and lead to economic growth and development.

The demand for environmental amenities is highly responsive to increases in income. It should not come as a surprise, therefore, that

Lomborg finds practically all environmental indicators improving through time as economic advance occurs.

The findings of this paper strongly corroborate the results from Antweiler, Copeland, and Taylor (2001) that international trade improves the natural environment. An international trading system facilitates the direct trading of such environmental goods as debt-for-nature swaps and pollution rights. Trade also facilitates the transfer of technologies, including those that economize on environmental goods. Compared with autarky, international trade also conserves the use of scarce natural resources, including those that are closely associated with environmental quality, such as wildlife habitat, wetlands, forests, and water. And the rules of the WTO do not encourage a "race to the bottom" in environmental quality, but rather protect the preferences of member nations to establish their own environmental standards.

Although there may be some workers who lose from trade liberalization as their protected status is diminished, the winners from trade greatly outnumber the losers. Indeed, after adjustments run their course, freer trade decreases inequality in the distribution of income in both developed and developing countries that trade with each other. In addition, in the end, the gains from open borders in goods, people, and information are broadly distributed among the people. Therefore, the critics who view foreign trade as a capitalist plot to exploit poor people in developing countries are simply wrong.

The political problem is that trade liberalization is fragile as those few who have been protected lose their privileged position. Strong pressures will be brought to maintain and enhance protection, and politicians enhance their own interests by responding to these pressures. The 2002 farm bill and the erection of new tariffs in lumber and steel are symptomatic of the continuing political struggle between protectionists and free traders. Fast-track authority has been hailed by the Bush administration as necessary to consummate new trade deals, and recent deals made by the Office of the Trade Representative seem to support this position.

Why is trade liberalization so strongly resisted when it is easily demonstrated that consumers' gains exceed producers' losses? The public-choice principle of "concentrated benefits and diffused costs" explains this political bias. The wealth and income interests of producers are highly concentrated, and it pays them to invest large sums in acquiring political favors in the form of protection. By contrast, the interests of individual consumers tend to be highly diffused across the entire population (every consumer may lose a little from a steel tariff or a sugar quota), and it is individually infeasible for them to organize to protect their interests. Additionally, because their individual interests in a specific trade barrier are generally small and diffused, consumers may be even unaware of its consequences. Still, the situation is far from hopeless. Understanding the overall gains from trade, including beneficial effects to the natural environment, will contribute at the margin to pressures for liberalization.

Another obstacle to free trade is the persistence in the world, including in the United States, of a "mercantilist" view of trade. Despite heroic efforts more than two centuries ago to rid the world of this malignancy, Adam Smith has not yet prevailed. Economists continue to advance the cause of trade liberalization but with only limited success. Even the argot of trade in current use seems perverse to the cause. Eliminating a trade barrier is referred to as a "concession" that requires "reciprocity" (*The Economist* 2001, 27). Nearly every person on the street believes that exports are good and imports bad. However, if consumption is the desired end of economic activity, then free trade is a goal that deserves universal support. Economists and other free traders have their work cut out for them to convince others of the merit of this objective.

Notes

1. Comparative advantage is one of the crown jewels of the economics profession. It has shaped the way economists view the world and serves as

the basis for the profession's overwhelming support of free trade (Rodrick 1998, 3).

2. Lomborg's credibility on environmental questions is attributable to two factors: (1) Lomborg's intent as a committed environmentalist was to debunk and disprove the ideas of economist Julian Simon, who had argued that many of the cherished mantras of the environmental community were demonstrably wrong; and (2) as a statistician, Lomborg is trained to evaluate data—their source, validity, and relevance. He also understands how models are constructed and the purpose of *ceteris paribus* assumptions in looking at complex problems. Because he is a statistician, Lomborg sees problems and their solutions in terms of stochastic probabilities rather than as the certitudes that have made modern environmentalism more a religion than a path of scientific inquiry.

References

Amsden, Alice. 2002. On globalism after 9/11: Let's give the third world a break. *The Milken Institute Review* (first quarter): 8–13.

Antweiler, Werner, Brian R. Copeland, and M. Scott Taylor. 2001. Is free trade good for the environment? *American Economic Review* 91 (September 4): 877–908.

Bhagwati, Jagdish. 2002. *Free Trade Today*. Princeton, N.J.: Princeton University Press.

Blustein, Paul. 2002. *The Chastening*. New York: Public Affairs.

Brown, Drusilla K., Alan V. Deardorff, and Robert M. Stern. 2001. Impacts on NAFTA members of multilateral and regional trade agreements and initiatives and harmonization of NAFTA's external tariffs. Research Seminar in International Economics Discussion Paper 471 (June). University of Michigan.

Chakravorty, Ujjayant, James Roumasset, and Kinping Tse. 1997. Endogenous substitution among energy resources and global warming. *Journal of Political Economy* 105 (6): 1201–34.

De Soto, Hernando. 2000. *The Mystery of Capital*. New York: Basic Books.

Deacon, Robert T., and Paul Murphy. 1993. Swapping debts for nature: Direct international trade in environmental services. In *NAFTA and the Environment*, ed. Terry L. Anderson. San Francisco: Pacific Research Institute for Public Policy Research, 69–90.

———. 1997. The structure of an environmental transaction: The debt-for-nature swap. *Land Economics* 73 (February 1): 1–24.

Eaton, Jonathan, and Samuel Kortum. 2001. Trade in capital goods. NBER Working Paper 8070 (January). Cambridge, Mass.: National Bureau of Economic Research.

The Economist. 2001. Globalization and its critics (September 29): 1–30.

The Economist. 2002a. Dangerous activities (May 11–17): 63–66.

The Economist. 2002b. The perils of packet switching (April 6): 13.

The Economist. 2002c. Promoting the noble cause of commerce (August 3): 57.

Frankel, Jeffrey A., and David Romer. 1999. Does trade cause growth? *American Economic Review* 89 (June): 379–99.

Friedman, Thomas L. 2000. *The Lexus and the olive tree.* New York: Anchor Books, Random House, Inc.

Gardner, B. Delworth. 1995. *Plowing ground in Washington.* San Francisco: Pacific Research Institute.

Globerman, Steven. 1993. The environmental impacts of trade liberalization. In *NAFTA and the Environment*, ed. Terry L. Anderson. San Francisco: Pacific Research Institute for Public Policy Research, 27–44.

Harrison, Glen W., Thomas F. Rutherford, and David G. Tarr. 1996. Quantifying the Uruguay round. In *The Uruguay Round and the Developing Countries*, ed. Will Martin and L. Alan Winters. New York: Cambridge University Press.

Heckscher, Eli F. 1949. The effects of foreign trade on the distribution of income. In *Readings in the Theory of International Trade*, ed. H. S. Ellis and L. A. Metzler. Philadelphia: Blakiston.

Irwin, Douglas A. 2002a. *Free trade under fire.* Princeton, N.J.: Princeton University Press.

———. 2002b. Free trade under fire. *The Milken Institute Review* (second quarter): 69–82.

Keller, Wolfgang. 2000. Do trade patterns and technology flows affect productivity growth? *World Bank Economic Review* 14 (January): 17–47.

Lindsey, Brink. 2002a. *Against the dead hand.* New York: John Wiley & Sons.

———. 2002b. Mixed signals on trade barriers. *Wall Street Journal*, July 30, A14.

Lomborg, Bjørn. 2001. *The skeptical environmentalist: Measuring the real state of the world.* New York: Cambridge University Press.

Micklethwait, John, and Adrian Wooldridge. 2002. Globalization goes upscale. *Wall Street Journal*, February 1, A14.

Nordhaus, William, and Joseph Boyer. 1999. Requiem for Kyoto: An economic analysis of the Kyoto Protocol. *The Energy Journal* (Kyoto special issue): 93–100.

Obstfeld, Maurice. 1998. The global capital market: Benefactor or menace? *Journal of Economic Perspectives* 12 (4, fall): 9–30.

Ohlin, B. 1933. Interregional and international trade. Cambridge, Mass.: Harvard University Press.

Patterson, J. H. 1993. Trade liberalization, agricultural policy, and wildlife: Reforming the landscape. In *NAFTA and the Environment*, ed. Terry L. Anderson. San Francisco: Pacific Research Institute for Public Policy Research, 61–68.

Perkins, Dwight H., Steven Radeler, Donald R. Snodgrass, Malcolm Gillis, and Michael Roemer. 2001. *Economics of development*. New York: W. W. Norton.

Ricardo, David. 1817. *On the principles of political economy and taxation*. London: John Murray.

Rodrik, Dani. 1997. Has globalization gone too far? Washington, D.C.: Institute for International Economics.

———. 1998. Symposium of globalization in perspective: An introduction. *Journal of Economic Perspectives* 12 (4, fall): 3–8.

Roland-Holst, David, Kenneth Reinhardt, and Clinton Schiells. 1992. North American trade liberalization and the role of nontariff barriers. In *Economywide Modeling of the economic implication of an FTA with Mexico and a NAFTA with Canada and Mexico*. USITC Publication 20436. Washington, D.C.: U.S. International Trade Commission.

Rushford, Greg. 2002. Fair trade: Does this emperor wear clothes? *Milken Review* (first quarter): 40–47.

Sachs, Jeffrey, and Andrew Warner. 1995. Economic reform and the process of global integration. *Brookings Papers on Economic Activity* 1: 1–95.

Stiglitz, Joseph E. 2002. *Globalization and its discontents*. New York: W. W. Norton.

Stolper, Wolfgang F., and Paul A. Samuelson. 1941. Protection and real wages. *Review of Economic Studies* 9 (November): 58–73.

Takayama, Ahiro. 1972. *International Trade*. New York: Holt, Rinehart, and Winston, Inc.

Thurow, Roger, and Scott Kilman. 2002. How a cotton glut bred by U.S. harms poor farmers abroad. *Wall Street Journal*, June 26, A1.

Wall Street Journal. 2002a. A free-trade revival. Editorial. August 15, A12.

Wall Street Journal. 2002b. Europe beats America. Editorial. July 23, A14.

World Bank Group. 2001a. Globalization, growth and poverty: Building an inclusive world economy. December 5. Online: http:// econ.worldbank.org/prr/globalization/.

———. 2001b. Launching "Development round" could help poor countries facing global downturn. News release 2002/111/S. October 31. Online: http://lnweb18.worldbank.org/news/pressrelease.nsf/Attachments/ pr103101eap.pdf/$File/pr103101eap.pdf.

World Trade Organization. 1999. The legal texts: The results of the Uruguay round of multilateral trade negotiations. New York: Cambridge University Press.

Yandle, Bruce. 1993. Is free trade an enemy of environmental quality? In *NAFTA and the Environment*, ed. Terry L. Anderson. San Francisco: Pacific Research Institute for Public Policy Research, 1–11.

Chapter 5

Population Growth, Economic Freedom, and the Rule of Law

Seth W. Norton

MORE THAN 200 YEARS AGO, the Reverend Thomas Malthus argued that people's tendency to have children would inevitably strain food supplies and limit the standard of living attainable by the mass of humanity. His pessimistic argument has proved remarkably durable, its influence ebbing and flowing through the ensuing centuries. In contemporary form, this contention has been expressed as a "Malthusian population trap" (Todaro 1996).

Malthus's idea was that the growth of human population keeps most people in society at a subsistence level of income. As income starts to go up, people produce more children, so the average (or per capita) income declines or stays at a low level. In the original Malthusian view, there were positive checks on population growth, but these were starvation, disease, and wars. Population growth was limited by the attendant mortality.

In today's neo-Malthusian perspective, preventive checks on pop-

Seth W. Norton is Aldeen professor of business at Wheaton College and a 2001 PERC Julian Simon Fellow. He holds a B.A. in history from Northwestern University and an M.B.A. in finance and a Ph.D. in economics from the University of Chicago.

ulation growth—persuasive and even coercive measures to lower birth rates—are required if people are to escape from mere subsistence living. Lester R. Brown, Gary Gardner, and Brian Halweil (1998, 71) illustrate this view:

> What is needed, to use a basketball term, is a full-court press—an all-out effort to lower fertility, particularly in the high-fertility countries, while there is still time. We see four key steps in doing this: undertaking national carrying-capacity assessments to help governments and the public at large to better understand the urgency of stabilizing population, filling the family planning gap, educating young women, and adopting a worldwide campaign to stop at two surviving children.

Not everyone shares a dread of population growth. In numerous books and articles, the late Julian Simon (1981, 1990, 1995) has documented benefits associated with population growth and has also shown that many apocalyptic nightmares are without foundation. In addition, Esther Boserup (1998 [1965]) took a favorable view of population growth when she said that in comparatively underdeveloped economies it induces technological change and stimulates innovation.

More recently, Bjørn Lomborg (2001) has provided a remarkable array of data showing that human well-being is improving. It is true that population growth is continuing worldwide, largely due to the lag in adjustments in birth rates that follow decreases in mortality rates. However, the striking fact is that mortality rates are declining, and decreased birth rates characteristically follow decreases in mortality rates. So although population growth rates may appear unusually high by long-run standards, the data merely reflect a demographic transition, and dramatic decreases in fertility rates are already evident in many countries. Most important, Lomborg shows that the potentially adverse effects of population growth are swamped by the ever-ubiquitous progress in so many avenues of life, including science, technology, and human productivity.

In spite of these contributions, most of the popular literature on the subject still echoes the Malthusian concerns. Lindsey Grant (1996, 3) provides a summary of popular sentiment:

> Population growth is leading us to a world that we do not want. It is the most fundamental of the engines of change, and the most ignored. The poor nations face sheer hunger and the destruction of their resources. The "emerging nations," most of them in Asia, are in varying degrees escaping those horrors to face the problems of industrialization. The old "rich" countries confront joblessness, failing social structures, growing disparities between the rich and poor, ethnic conflict, the loss of a shared vision, environmental degradation, and the huge reality that they are changing the climate we all live in. Bringing population growth under control will not necessarily solve those problems, but it is the condition precedent—a necessary condition for their solution.

In this chapter, I address the topic of population somewhat differently. For the purpose of analysis, I accept the received knowledge among prominent policy-makers and cultural elites that population growth has adverse effects that could be quite severe. This neo-Malthusian view will serve as a point of departure for analysis to determine its validity and its policy relevance.

My analysis introduces the role of economic institutions, which so far has been much ignored in discussions of population growth. By *economic institutions*, I mean the formal and informal customs, laws, and traditions that guide behavior. A burgeoning body of research shows that several key institutions—economic freedom, protection of property rights, and the rule of law—are closely linked to human well-being. Consequently, it is reasonable to expect that such institutions can ameliorate population problems.

This chapter reviews several aspects of the so-called population problem, with the goal of shedding light on whether economic institutions affect population growth and, more important, whether they affect conditions, such as poverty and environmental degradation, that population growth is supposed to cause. First, I examine the simple effects of population growth on human well-being. Second, I look at the role of growth-enhancing institutions as capable of offsetting any adverse effects of population growth. Third, I compare the net effects of population growth and economic institutions on poverty and the environment. Fourth, I look at the effect of economic institutions on fertility. Finally, I calculate the effects of modest institutional reforms on human well-being.

Alleged Adverse Effects of Population Growth

Some observers attribute nearly all of the world's maladies to excessive population growth. More specifically, they claim that population growth has at least three adverse effects on human well-being. First, it increases the number of people that are impoverished, the proportion of the community that is impoverished, and the severity of the impoverishment. Second, it increases environmental degradation—the misuse of natural resources, with adverse consequences on many dimensions of human well-being. And finally, it prevents environmental enhancement by holding back the savings and investment that would permit environmentally sustainable economic growth and retards the agricultural productivity that would encourage environmentally friendly agriculture and conservation (Ahlburg 1994; Kelley and McGreevey 1994).

These assertions can be specified in greater detail and related to widely held assertions among policy makers as well as notable proportions in the scientific and economic communities. However, it should be noted that the negative or apocalyptic views of population growth are far more common among policy makers than economists, and it was policy makers and bureaucrats who ignored or distorted the less pessimistic evidence generated by serious economic analysis (Kelley and McGreevey 1994; Kelley and Schmidt 1996). However, given the wide support for apocalyptic views, a closer look at the details of these assertions is warranted.

Poverty

A core idea of the Malthusian legacy is that population growth depresses wages because it increases the supply of workers and thus directly lowers the wages of workers. Depressed wages are likely to be particularly onerous for the poor because labor earnings constitute the main source of income for the poor, who are less likely to own other income-generating assets, such as land (Kelley and McGreevey 1994).

In addition, the argument continues, population growth strains investment as an economy strives to absorb workers by reducing savings, the supply of funds for investing in capital that will spur economic growth over the long run. This view has been developed in elegant models of economic growth, as in the acclaimed Solow (1956) growth model. Of course, proponents of this view recognize that technological advances or investment can accommodate population growth, but neo-Malthusians argue that the accommodation is more the exception than the rule.

It also merits noting that the neo-Malthusians view poverty as more than income deprivation. Rapid population growth strains the fixed capacities for basic human services such as education, health, and nutrition. Fixed levels of basic infrastructures that are essential for survival and longevity are spread over greater numbers of people and hence the per capita delivery of services is reduced. In short, nonpecuniary measures of poverty also increase (Ahlburg 1994).

Resource Depletion

Some observers claim that resources are harvested at excessive rates due to population pressure (Todaro 1996). The contention is that timber is harvested too quickly in order to supply such products as wood for housing construction. This depletes forests and causes additional environmental problems, such as soil erosion. More generally, the impoverishing effects of population growth make the populace excessively dependent on natural resource–based activities such as timber production.

Deforestation can cause soil erosion, watershed instability, and loss of carbon sequestration. Agricultural productivity also may fall. Moreover, the poor, it is said, bear a disproportionate part of the costs of deforestation. Deforestation can cause fuel supplies to dwindle, and the resulting costs of more extensive wood gathering are thought to be borne disproportionately by women (Todaro 1996).

Soil erosion, threats to marine ecology, and water pollution are commonly thought to be negative consequences of rapid population growth. Water pollution is often considered the most serious pollution. Todaro (1996) claims that water pollution and water scarcity lead to about two million deaths per year.

Net Savings

Another alleged harm of population growth is reduced savings. Population growth, it is said, diverts resources to child raising and consumption, reducing the proportion of the populace that is engaged in production and reducing the fraction of output that is saved and invested. Modern theories of consumption over the life cycle hold that population growth increases dependency ratios and in turn reduces savings (Kelley 1988). That is, a larger proportion of growing populations is under the age of fifteen. This group has a lower savings rate than adults between the ages of fifteen and sixty-four (Todaro 1996).

Agricultural Productivity

Agricultural productivity permits greater specialization in an economy and generates greater food supplies, but rapid population growth may keep productivity low, depressing wages and keeping people on marginal farms. Indeed, stagnation of agriculture and the failure to adopt innovative technology represent the basic Malthusian apocalypse. There is ample evidence of insufficient agricultural productivity in relatively poor countries, with corresponding adverse effects on poverty rates and the environment (Todaro 1996).

Evidence of Adverse Effects

To determine how much effect rapid population growth has in these areas, I examine ten specific features of human well-being. Because most of the assertions regarding the adverse effects of population growth pertain to poor countries, the measures are for a sample of countries that are categorized as "developing" by the United Nations (U.N.). The countries consist of those for whom the U.N. has calculated the Human Poverty Index. With few exceptions, one of which is Singapore, the countries are comparatively poor. (The well-being measures are described in more detail in the appendix at the end of this chapter.)

These are the specific indicators of well-being:

Poverty Measures

- United Nations Human Poverty Index
- Proportion of the population not expected to survive to age forty
- Proportion of the adult population that is illiterate
- Proportion of the population without access to safe water
- Proportion of the population without access to health services
- Proportion of the children under age five that are malnourished

Environmental Degradation

- Deforestation
- Water pollution

Table 5.1
Population Growth and Human Well-Being

Measure of Well-Being	POPULATION GROWTH: SHORT TERM			POPULATION GROWTH: LONG TERM		
	Low	Medium	High	Low	Medium	High
U.N. Human Poverty Index	19.3	32.8	34.1	19.6	34.6	25.7
Death by 40	12.6	22.0	22.2	10.9	23.7	16.1
Adult illiteracy	17.9	37.5	38.4	20.6	38.6	32.1
Safe water	23.8	36.1	34.4	28.3	38.4	19.3
Health services	20.8	27.7	37.2	17.9	31.4	21.6
Undernourished children	17.6	23.6	24.3	15.9	25.8	15.5
Deforestation rate	0.320	1.027	0.800	0.727	1.051	0.336
Water pollution	0.209	0.211	0.219	0.214	0.211	0.209
Net savings rate	9.2	5.4	4.0	10.0	4.3	8.8
Agricultural productivity	2,322.3	1,592.8	613.1	2,471.0	1,449.5	1,137.3

Sources: United Nations Development Program (1997); World Bank (2001)

Environmental Enhancement

- Agricultural productivity
- Savings

Table 5.1 contains the average levels for the poverty and environmental degradation and enhancement measures. The measures are calculated for high, medium, and low population growth rates for the short term (1985–1990) and the long term (1970–1990). Examples of countries with high population growth rates are Botswana, Kenya, and United Arab Emirates. Examples of countries with low population growth rates are China, Jamaica, and Mauritius. (A complete list of countries, for both the short term and the long term, is in the appendix.[1])

The data provide some basis for a neo-Malthusian interpretation. Consider the measure for the fraction of the population not surviving to the age of 40. Citizens in countries with low short-term population growth rates are about 10 percent more likely to survive to age 40 than those countries with high short-term population growth rates (12.6 in column 1 versus 22.2 in column 3). Savings rates are likewise substantially higher in countries with low short-term population growth rates than in those with high short-term growth rates. In the same vein, deforestation rates are higher in countries with high short-term population growth rates. The pattern is common—higher short-term population growth generates negative effects.

However, there are some data in Table 5.1 that do not support the neo-Malthusian view.[2] The gap between medium and high short-term growth rates is often very small. For example, in the death by 40 measure, the high and medium short-term population growth rates differ by only two-tenths (22.2 in column 3 versus 22.0 in column 2). In two measures—access to safe water and the rate of deforestation—the high population growth rate countries are actually better off than the medium growth rate countries.

When the measures of well-being are compared based on long-term population growth rates, the evidence supporting the neo-Malthusian view is even weaker. For a number of measures—the poverty index, under age 40 mortality, adult illiteracy, safe water, health services, undernourished children, the deforestation rate, water pollution, and the net savings rate—the well-being of citizens in high population growth rate countries exceeds the level for citizens in countries with medium population growth rates and, in the case of access to safe water, undernourished children, deforestation, and water pollution, the well-being of citizens in high population growth countries exceeds that of citizens in low population growth countries. In short, the data indicate that whatever ill effects population growth rate engenders, they are primarily tied in to short-term population growth rates.

Economic Institutions and Human Well-Being

There is growing evidence that many of the differences in well-being across countries are directly attributable to the quality of economic institutions—the existence of property rights, the quality of government, the rule of law, and economic freedom. The evidence is closely linked to the development in recent years of standard measures of institutional quality, developed so that countries can be compared based on these measures and on measures of well-being, such as income and mortality. Two of the more prominent measures are the rule of law and economic freedom.

Countries with a strong legal framework are typically distinguished from countries where the law reflects political struggles for power. Countries with a well-established tradition of the rule of law have greater ability to carry out business transactions (Barro and Sala-i-Martin 1995, 439) and correspondingly greater incentives for investment (Hirshleifer 1987, 53). Knack and Keefer (1995) say that the rule of law "reflects the degree to which the citizens of a country are willing to accept the established institutions to make and implement laws and adjudicate disputes."

A company called Political Risk Services ranks countries as part of its *International Country Risk Guide* (1997). Customers use the guide to make decisions about investment and production in foreign countries. In the rule-of-law rankings, higher scores indicate sound political institutions, a strong court system, and provisions for orderly succession of power. Lower scores indicate a tradition of depending on physical force or illegal means to settle claims. Using this database, research by Knack and Keefer (1995) and Barro and Sala-i-Martin (1995) shows that the rule of law enhances economic growth and human well-being.[3]

Economic freedom also enhances growth. The *Index of Economic Freedom* is a comprehensive measure of citizens' rights to own and trade property unfettered by intrusive public policies. The Fraser Institute compiles this index with the assistance of numerous organizations throughout the world.[4] Essentially, the project measures economic freedom as distinguished from political freedom. It emphasizes the ability of people to use and exchange property relatively free of governmental interference in the form of perverse monetary, fiscal, and trade policies (Gwartney, Lawson, and Block 1996; Gwartney and Lawson, 2000).

A recent compilation by Gwartney and Lawson (2001) ranks countries based on seven broad categories of economic freedom. These are the size of government, the economic structure and role of markets, monetary policy and price stability, freedom to use alternative currencies, the legal structure and security of private ownership, freedom to trade with foreigners, and freedom of exchange in capital markets. These measures, which are composed of twenty-one narrower yardsticks, are used to compile a summary measure of economic freedom for each country.

The role of economic institutions on human well-being can be examined by dividing the sample of countries into groups with low, medium, and high economic freedom and the same categories for the rule of law. It merits noting that because the sample countries are "developing," many of the countries of the world with the highest levels of economic freedom and rule of law are excluded. (That fact in itself says much about economic institutions and the standards of well-being across the world.) Consequently, countries with high economic freedom or strong rule of law would not qualify as such based on total world standards. For example, Chile, Panama, and Singapore all have high economic freedom in this sample. In a broader sample, Chile and Panama would not be viewed as having high economic freedom, although Singapore would. Similarly, China, Cuba, and Namibia are classified as having strong rule-of-law measures. By broader world standards, that conclusion seems questionable. The fact is that the sample of developing countries includes many with abysmal levels of economic freedom—Algeria, Myanmar, the Syrian Arab Republic—or abysmal levels of the rule of law—Bangladesh, Iraq, Peru. (A list of the high and low economic freedom and rule-of-law countries is in the appendix.) Consequently, the comparison is often among countries that exhibit less than ideal institutions.

Table 5.2 contains the measures of human well-being in those

Table 5.2
Economic Institutions and Human Well-Being

Measure of Well-Being	ECONOMIC FREEDOM			RULE OF LAW		
	Low	Medium	High	Low	Medium	High
U.N. Human Poverty Index	38.1	30.5	14.5	31.8	33.0	16.4
Death by 40	29.1	19.4	7.7	19.6	21.7	10.8
Adult illiteracy	39.2	34.7	12.5	32.1	37.8	17.0
Safe water	43.3	34.7	19.5	34.8	36.2	20.1
Health services	40.5	28.5	16.8	41.3	28.0	15.2
Undernourished children	29.1	21.7	13.9	25.0	23.1	14.0
Deforestation rate	0.429	1.351	−0.230	1.336	0.732	0.282
Water pollution	0.200	0.214	0.196	0.202	0.221	0.194
Net savings rates	3.96	7.12	14.78	2.61	6.30	15.96
Agricultural productivity	620.3	1,011.2	6,001.6	1,178.2	1,083.6	4,552.7

Sources: Gwartney and Lawson (2001); Political Risk Services (1997); United Nations Development Program (1997); World Bank (2001)

groups of countries. In all cases except water pollution, countries with low economic freedom are worse off than those in countries with moderate economic freedom, whereas in all cases those in countries with high economic freedom were better off than those in countries with medium economic freedom. By these measures, quality of life is strongly linked to economic freedom.[5]

For the rule-of-law measures, a similar pattern is evident. Well-being is better for citizens in countries with moderate rule of law as opposed to weak rule of law, except for the overall poverty index, adult illiteracy, and agricultural productivity. For citizens in countries with strong rule of law, well-being is uniformly better than in countries with medium rule of law. Thus, the relationship for rule of law is not as strong as economic freedom, but by many measures of the quality of life, life is better when the rule of law is stronger.

Table 5.3
Effects of Changing Population Growth Versus
Effects of Changing Economic Institutions

Measure of Well-Being	POPULATION GROWTH GAP: HIGH MINUS LOW		INSTITUTIONAL GAP: HIGH MINUS LOW	
	Short Run	*Long Run*	*Economic Freedom*	*Rule of Law*
U.N. Human Poverty Index	14.8	6.1	−23.6	−15.4
Death by 40	9.6	5.2	−21.4	−8.8
Adult illiteracy	20.5	11.5	−26.7	−15.1
Safe water	10.6	−9.0	−23.8	−14.7
Health services	16.4	3.7	−23.7	−26.1
Undernourished children	6.7	−0.5	−15.2	−11.0
Deforestation rate	0.480	−0.391	−0.659	−1.054
Water pollution	0.010	−0.005	−0.004	−0.008
Net savings rates	−5.24	−1.25	10.82	13.35
Agricultural productivity	−1,709	−1,334	5,381	3,375

Note: The gap for rule of law is strong rule of law minus weak rule of law.
Sources: Gwartney and Lawson (2001); Political Risk Services (1997); United Nations Development Program (1997); World Bank (2001)

Effects of Population Growth and Economic Institutions

One of the difficulties in drawing conclusions from basic statistics is that the role of other factors is easily ignored. For example, the data in Table 5.1 do not reflect differences in economic institutions. A constructive comparison examines the relative effects of population growth and economic institutions on the measures of human well-being. Table 5.3 compares the gap between the high and low categories for both population growth and economic institutions.[6] The data are shown for each of the ten measures of human well-being. For example, the first entry for the under-40 mortality rate (row 2, column 1) is 9.6. The number is the percentage of the population not surviving in countries with high short-term population growth minus the percentage of people not surviving in countries with low short-term population growth (22.2 − 12.6). The same line for the institutional gap shows the gap (−21.4) between high and low economic freedom countries (7.7 − 29.1). A higher difference means that economic freedom has a greater effect in reducing mortality than comparable population growth has in increasing mortality.

The data in Table 5.3 show two patterns. First, there is the effect documented in Table 5.1—that whatever adverse effects population growth generates, they are always more noticeable in the short term than the long term. Indeed, in several cases—undernourished children, deforestation, water pollution—higher long-term population growth is associated with enhanced well-being.

Second, the beneficial effects of moving from low economic freedom to high economic freedom or from weak rule of law to strong rule of law exceed any harmful effects of increased population growth. The pattern holds for all measures of human well-being except the water pollution measure, where the benefits fall just short of offsetting the harmful effects. In many cases—for example, the under-40 mortality rate or the net savings rate—the numbers are striking. Simply stated, economic institutions are more important than population growth in terms of these measures of human well-being.

The data in Table 5.3 may overstate the harmful effects of population growth because the adverse effects of population growth could be confused with other factors. Clearly, rapid population growth often occurs along with other forces that reduce human well-being (Kelley 1988; Panayotou 1994). For example, rapid population growth is common in many tropical areas of the world. Yet tropical environments retard human productive activity because of heat, endemic disease, and poor soils (Sachs and Warner 1997). It would be easy to conclude that lower productivity is caused by fast population growth when the tropical environment may be the cause.

Where multiple factors determine various outcomes, it is difficult to distinguish cause and effect without simultaneously considering the

Table 5.4

Net Effects of Changes in Population Growth Versus
Changes in Economic Institutions

| Measure of Well-Being | POPULATION GROWTH | | ECONOMIC INSTITUTIONS | |
	Short Term	Long Term	Economic Freedom	Rule of Law
U.N. Human Poverty Index	0.445	0.186	−0.812	−0.449
Death by 40	0.520	0.415	−0.973	−0.386
Adult illiteracy	0.764	0.596	−0.731	−0.386
Safe water	0.000	0.000	−1.043	−0.450
Health services	0.783	0.000	−1.030	−0.105
Undernourished children	0.000	0.000	0.000	0.000
Deforestation rate	0.000	0.000	0.000	−1.052
Water pollution	0.000	0.000	0.000	−0.256
Net savings rate	0.000	0.000	3.160	1.802
Agricultural productivity	0.000	0.000	1.640	0.000

Note: The numbers represent the percentage change in the measure of well-being owing to comparable changes in population or economic institutions after accounting for landlocked and tropical conditions and the degree of urbanization.

Sources: Gwartney and Lawson (2001); Political Risk Services (1997); United Nations Development Program (1997); World Bank (2001)

effects of other variables. Modern statistical analysis permits analysis that "nets out" the effects of other variables.[7] Using such analysis yields estimates of the effects of population growth on the measure of well-being after netting out the impact of a country being landlocked, tropical, urbanized, and, most important, economically free. Similar analysis can yield the net effects of economic institutions on human well-being after accounting for the effects of population growth, tropical climates, and urbanization. The net effects of population growth, economic freedom, and the rule of law on the well-being measures are highlighted in Table 5.4.

The numbers in columns 1 and 2 represent the effect of a percentage change in short-term population growth on the percentage changes in well-being measures and the comparable effect of long-term population growth. All the entries in both columns are less than 1.0, which means that an increase in population growth results in less than a proportionate reduction in the various measures of well-being. Moreover, the magnitudes are greater for the short-term population growth than for the long-term growth, a result that is consistent with Tables 5.1 and 5.3. More important, the effects for all the nonpoverty variables are zero. In essence, when we net out the effects of other influences—economic institutions, tropical climates, and urbanization—there is no evident harm from population growth.

Thus, the data in Tables 5.1 and 5.3 clearly overstate the negative effects of population growth. That conclusion holds for both the short term and the long term. Although the sample is restricted, it includes the most impoverished nations of the world, which are thought to be the most vulnerable to the adverse effects of population growth. The data support at worst a modest and more generally a nonexistent neo-Malthusian world.

The data in columns 3 and 4 of Table 5.4 are in sharp contrast to columns 1 and 2. Increases in economic freedom or the rule of law reduce poverty, reduce deforestation and water pollution, and increase savings and agricultural productivity. Thus, unlike population effects, economic institutions are significant when other factors, such as climate and urbanization, are appropriately considered. Economic freedom tends to dominate rule of law in terms of magnitude of effects, but there are exceptions, such as deforestation or water pollution where the rule of law improves the environment but economic freedom does not. And finally, it merits noting that, as shown in the data presented in Table 5.3, the (absolute) magnitude of the institutional effect (the strongest of the economic freedom or rule of law effect) dominates the magnitude of the population effect. The only exception is adult illiteracy, where the short-term population effect slightly exceeds the economic freedom effect. Thus, the net effects show that institutional reform would more than offset the adverse effects of population growth.

Effect of Institutions on Fertility

The data in the previous section show that economic institutions are dramatically more important than population growth in affecting human poverty and environmental conditions and that the combined effects of economic institutions and population growth render the latter as fairly benign. However, those conclusions still understate the importance of economic institutions with respect to population growth because economic institutions actually affect fertility rates, and hence population growth rates. (Fertility rates are birth rates adjusted for the age composition of the population.)

There are ample grounds to believe people will adjust their fertility, that is increase or reduce the number of children they bear, in light of their human endowments and opportunities. Economists Gary Becker and Robert Barro (1988) have developed a model of human fertility indicating that people choose the number of children in response to changing mortality rates while taking into account the forgone opportunities associated with raising children. If people anticipate that many of their children will die before reaching adulthood, they will have more children. If they are confident that their children, or most of them, will reach adulthood, they will have fewer children. In both cases, they will also consider the costs of lost income and lost free time that occur when raising children. Becker and Barro argue that as education and work experience of females increase and open up more productive opportunities for women, the costs of raising children will increase.

Another reason the costs of having children can increase as income increases is that economic growth depends in large part on increased skills and productivity and specialization. To become productive as adults in developed countries, children must have more education and higher skill levels than those in countries with static economies. Thus, economic growth can be expected to reduce fertility, both because of the higher opportunity costs on the part of the parents and because of the longer and more expensive education required for the children.

It also is true that higher incomes permit people to raise more children, so economic growth could have the opposite effect. Empirical evidence, however, suggests that as economic growth occurs, fertility rates rise only for the poorest segments of the population. For income levels above the poorest, economic growth leads to lower fertility rates (Barro and Sala-i-Martin 1995). Given the link between economic growth and fertility, institutions that encourage economic growth should also encourage reduced fertility.

A simple relationship between economic freedom and rule of law measures and fertility is shown in Table 5.5, using a large sample of countries for which both the fertility rate and the two institutional measures are available (109 countries for the economic freedom measure; 129 countries for the rule of law measure). The countries are divided into three categories for both economic freedom and rule of law. The fertility rate is highest for those countries that have little economic freedom and little respect for the rule of law.[8]

The relationship is a powerful one. Fertility rates are more than twice as high in countries with low levels of economic freedom and rule of law compared with countries that have high levels of those measures. Formal analysis of the data indicates that these differences are not merely random.[9]

The link between these institutions and fertility partly reflects the impact of economic growth—by encouraging economic growth, these institutions indirectly affect fertility. But there also is evidence that these growth-enhancing institutions affect fertility for other reasons. Many developing countries have poorly specified or poorly enforced property rights. When fuel wood and fodder are not owned and formal laws of possession do not govern their harvest and use, people do not bear the full cost of their consumption. They have an incentive to appropriate resources at the fastest rate possible, often leading to excessive harvest. This condition is generally labeled the "tragedy of the commons." What better way to capture open-access resources than to have as many gatherers as possible? Higher fertility is a way to do this.

Table 5.5
Economic Institutions and Fertility Rates

Institutional Measure	Fertility Rates		
Economic freedom	*Low Freedom* 4.27	*Medium Freedom* 3.27	*High Freedom* 1.82
Rule of law	*Weak Law* 4.16	*Medium Law* 3.53	*Strong Law* 1.55

Note: Total fertility rate is the number of children that would be born to a woman if she were to live to the end of her childbearing years and bear children at each age in accordance with the prevailing age-specific fertility rates. Fertility rates are for 1999.
Sources: Gwartney and Lawson (2001); Political Risk Services (1997); World Bank (2001)

Theodore Panayotou (1994, 151) observes that "most contributions by children consist of capturing and appropriating open-access natural resources such as water, fodder, pastures, fish, fuel wood, and other forest products, and clearing open-access land for cultivation." This, he continues, makes "the number of children the decisive instrument in the hands of the household: The household's share of open-access property depends on the number of hands it employs to convert open-access resources into private property." Yet this could "become devastating for the resource, the community, and eventually the individual household."

The absence of economic freedom encourages fertility in another way, too. Arthur De Vany and Nicolas Sanchez (1979) examined fertility patterns in Mexico based on the proportion of private farms and *ejido* farms—communally owned farms organized under the laws enacted following the Revolution of 1910. In addition to incentives to have children in order to appropriate resources, they assert there are incentives to have children in order to transfer property. Because of restrictions on sales of land, many people have the right to use but not sell the land. They can obtain some benefits of selling the land by transferring it to their progeny. More children increase the ability to make such transfers. On farms without clear ownership, the parents with more children will have a greater chance of at least some children taking over the farm and providing for the parents in their old age.

Finally, there may be a simple pronatalist bias to obtain "free" family farm labor. Not surprisingly, De Vany and Sanchez found that the higher the proportion of *ejidatarios* (workers on communal farms) relative to women or to total farm workers, the higher the fertility. In short, fertility and favorable economic institutions are inversely related. Where property rights are poorly defined and enforced, the incentives to have children are greater than where property rights are well specified and enforced.

Additional confirmation of the link between poorly protected property rights and high fertility comes from two measures produced as part of the Political Risk Service's *International Country Risk Guide*. Comprehensive and standardized measures of land-ownership patterns across countries are not as available as the economic freedom and rule of law measures, but two indices can serve as proxies for ill-defined property rights in land. One index ranks countries by the likelihood that contracts will be broken, and the other by the likelihood that their governments will expropriate property. Knack and Keefer (1995) describe the first measure as the "risk of modification of contract in the form of repudiation, postponement, or scaling down due to budget cutbacks, indigenization pressure, a change in government, or a change in government economic or social priorities." The second is an assessment of "outright confiscation" or "forced nationalization" of property.

Table 5.6 compares fertility rates for relatively poor countries depending on whether they have strong or weak institutions. The sample contains those countries with per capita GDP in 1995 beneath the average (1,579 US$) for the group of countries used in Table 5.1. The countries are divided into those below average and those above average for honoring contracts and not expropriating property. In the weak category are countries where contracts are less likely to be honored and where property is more likely to be expropriated; in the strong category

Table 5.6

Economic Institutions and Fertility Rates: Poor Countries

Institutional Measure	TOTAL FERTILITY RATE	
	Weak Institutions	*Strong Institutions*
Honoring contracts	4.88	3.68
Expropriation risk	4.62	3.22

Note: Total fertility rate is the number of children that would be born to a woman if she were to live to the end of her childbearing years and bear children at each age in accordance with the prevailing age-specific fertility rates. The fertility rates are for 1999.

Sources: Political Risk Services (1997); World Bank (2001)

are countries where contracts are more likely to be honored and where property is less likely to be expropriated.

Fertility rates are notably lower in the countries that have a tradition of honoring contracts and not expropriating property. These numbers are remarkable because they show that even among the poorer countries of the world, security of contractual relations and the protection of private property tend to lower fertility rates.

When the capture of open-access resources is rendered unnecessary by a system of laws that assigns full ownership and the ability to transfer property, families do not need so many children.

Institutional Reform and Population Growth

The data in Tables 5.1–5.6 build a compelling case for institutional reform as the means to solve problems that are often erroneously attributed to population growth. There are two reasons to advocate institutional reform. First, nations that adopt growth-enhancing reforms, such as better protection of property rights and acceptance of the rule of law, improve people's lives. Favorable economic institutions directly decrease human poverty and environmental degradation and enhance the environment, improving conditions even in realms where population growth has little effect.

Second, economic freedom, the rule of law, and related market-enhancing institutions also reduce fertility rates, as discussed earlier and shown in Table 5.5. By reducing population growth, they reduce any adverse consequences of population growth.

To illustrate the effects of these institutions, I have constructed a table showing hypothetical changes in the measurements of well-being if economic freedom were increased from low to medium or medium to high levels or comparable changes for the rule of law measure as shown in Tables 5.2–5.4. These direct effects are based on estimates of the relationship between the poverty and environmental measures and economic freedom and the rule of law.[10]

Using the information in Table 5.5, I calculate the indirect effects on human well-being that would derive from lower fertility rates resulting from modest institutional reforms. Going from low to medium economic freedom would lower the fertility rate from 4.27 to 3.27, or one child per woman of childbearing age. Going from medium to high economic freedom would lower the total fertility rate from 3.27 to 1.82, or by 1.45 children. Using the average of the two, approximately 1.2 children per woman of childbearing age, I calculate the degree to which some of the measures, such as adult illiteracy, would fall.

Thus, using the data reported in Table 5.4 (the sensitivity of measures of well-being to population growth), it is possible to calculate the decrease in human poverty measures caused by lower fertility rates. (Recall that lower fertility rates did not affect the environmental factors.) The decreases in poverty measures constitute the indirect effects of institutional reform.

Table 5.7 contains the combined direct and indirect effects. The first column of numbers contains the average levels of the well-being measures for the sample countries. For example, the average fraction of the population that fails to survive to age 40 is 20.8 percent. The last column shows the new average that would result from a modest

Table 5.7
Hypothetical Effects of Modest Institutional Reforms

Measure	Average	Direct Effects	Indirect Effects	Reformed Value
U.N. Human Poverty Index	31.01	−5.99	−5.17	19.85
Death by 40	20.84	−4.82	−4.06	11.96
Adult illiteracy	35.14	−6.11	−10.07	18.96
Safe water	34.29	−8.51	—	25.78
Health services	28.14	−10.26	−8.14	9.74
Undernourished children	22.92	—	—	22.92
Deforestation rate	0.902	−0.329	—	0.573
Water pollution	0.212	−0.019	—	0.193
Net savings rate	5.64	4.78	—	10.42
Agricultural productivity	1,564	610.46	—	2,174

Note: The numbers in column 2 are the averages for the measures in column 1. The direct effects are the results from increasing economic freedom (rule of law) from low (weak) to medium or from medium to high (strong) after netting out the effects of other variables. The indirect effects are the results from lower fertility rates that accompany comparable institutional reforms.

Sources: Gwartney and Lawson (2001); Political Risk Services (1997); United Nations Development Program (1997); World Bank (2001)

improvement in either the Economic Freedom of the World Index or the rule of law measure.[11] The results combine the direct and indirect effects of reform.

To see this more clearly, consider the effects of modest institutional reform—an increase in economic freedom from the levels in Colombia or Togo to the levels of Paraguay or Guatemala or an increase in the rule of law measure from the levels in El Salvador or Nigeria to the levels in Egypt or India. The proportion of people not surviving to age 40 would fall to about 12 percent of the population, compared with nearly 21 percent. Similarly, institutional reform would lower the proportion of illiterate adults from 35 percent of the population to just under 19 percent. A modest reform of the rule of law would reduce the deforestation rate to just under 0.6 percent, a notable decrease. Reform would increase the savings rate from about 5.64 percent to more than 10 percent and raise agricultural productivity from an average of $1,564 (in 1995 US$) to $2,174.

Conclusion

The data presented above lead to four simple conclusions:

- Adverse effects of population growth are small.
- Economic institutions can offset the adverse effects of population growth.
- Market-enhancing economic institutions lower fertility rates.
- Reforming institutions is far more important than controlling population growth.

There is no population apocalypse. Institutional reform can largely offset any population problems, both directly, by improving well-being, and indirectly, by leading to lower fertility rates. Moreover, the results understate the potential benefits of institutional reform because the sample excludes countries in which economic institutions are substantially more supportive of human well-being. Reforming economic freedom to Hong Kong's level or the rule of law to Switzerland's level would surely have substantially greater impact on human well-being. In short, there is considerable basis for optimism.

Yet, despite these findings, there is also considerable room for pessimism. Institutional reform is not free. Numerous nation-states, for various reasons, resist the kind of reform that would ameliorate population problems in particular and human problems in general. This state of affairs is perplexing and troubling. Perhaps the evidence documented here will be used in the debates to help policy makers take action to reform the institutional environment and thus the most basic building blocks of human well-being—markets and growth-enhancing institutions.

Notes

1. The high and low categories refer to countries that are one standard deviation above or below the average (mean). The standard deviation is a conventional measure of dispersion. For normally distributed populations, the interval around the mean would be about 68 percent of the population, and the high and low categories would collectively constitute about 32 percent of the population.

2. For the reader familiar with rudimentary statistical inference, the most compelling evidence against the neo-Malthusian view is that the gap between the high population growth and medium population growth is never both adverse and statistically significant. For nonpoverty measures, the low growth and medium growth difference is not significant in any case except long-run population growth and undernourished children. In that case, however, the proportion of children that are undernourished is lower in the higher-population-growth group.

3. The data were compiled by Political Risk Services (now PRS Group) but were obtained from the Center for Institutional Reform and the Informal Sector (IRIS) at the University of Maryland.

4. The research is discussed in Gwartney, Lawson, and Block (1996) as part of the Economic Freedom Project and by Easton and Walker (1997).

5. The gap between low economic freedom and medium economic freedom is statistically significant for the poverty index, death by age 40, health service, and undernourished children. The gap between high economic freedom and medium economic freedom is statistically significant for all measures except health service and water pollution. For the rule of law, the gap between weak and medium is not statistically significant, but the gap between medium and strong is significant for all but undernourished children and water pollution. However, statistical significance is not a powerful concept unless other factors are also considered. See Table 5.4.

6. For population growth, the statistically significant gaps are the poverty index, death by age 40, and adult illiteracy. All others are not significant. The measured gaps are all significant except for deforestation rates and water pollution for economic freedom, and water pollution and agricultural productivity for the rule of law. The caveat regarding other confounding factors applies here as well.

7. The estimation procedure is the well-established multiple regression technique common in economics and other sciences. The ordinary least-squares technique was used in the estimates. Zero entries represent esti-

mates that are not statistically significant. Unlike the simple averages in Tables 5.1–5.3, statistical significance is crucial here because the effects of other forces—for example, tropical climates—are included in the estimates.

8. The full sample of countries, not just the United Nation's sample of developing countries, is used for this table.

9. In the language of statistics, the gaps are statistically significant well beyond the 99 percent confidence level.

10. For the original estimates, see Norton (2001).

11. The modest improvement is a one-standard-deviation increase in economic freedom or the rule of law.

References

Ahlburg, Dennis. 1994. Population growth and poverty. In *Population and development: Old debates, new conclusions*, ed. Robert Cassen. New Brunswick, N.J.: Transactions Publishers.

Barro, Robert J., and Xavier Sala-i-Martin. 1995. *Economic growth*. New York: McGraw-Hill.

Becker, Gary, and Robert J. Barro. 1988. A reformulation of the economic theory of fertility. *Quarterly Journal of Economics* 103: 1–25.

Boserup, Esther. 1998 [1965]. *The conditions of agricultural growth*. London: Earthscan.

Brown, Lester R., Gary Gardner, and Brian Halweil. 1998. *Beyond Malthus*. Washington, D.C.: Worldwatch Institute.

De Vany, Arthur, and Nicolas Sanchez. 1979. Land tenure structures and fertility in Mexico. *Review of Economics and Statistics* 61: 67–72.

Easton, Stephen, and Michael Walker. 1997. Income, growth, economic freedom. *American Economic Review* 87: 328–32.

Grant, Lindsey. 1996. *Juggernaut*. Santa Ana, Calif.: Seven Locks Press.

Gwartney, James, and Robert Lawson. 2000. *Economic freedom of the world*. Vancouver: Fraser Institute.

———. 2001. *Economic freedom of the world*. Vancouver: Fraser Institute.

Gwartney, James, Robert Lawson, and Walter Block. 1996. *Economic freedom of the world*. Vancouver: Fraser Institute.

Hirshleifer, Jack. 1987. *Economic behavior in adversity*. Chicago: University of Chicago Press.

Kelley, Allen C. 1988. Economic consequences of population change in the third world. *Journal of Economic Literature* 26: 1685–1728.

———, and Paul McGreevey. 1994. Population and development in historical perspective. In *Population and development: Old debates, new conclusions*, ed. Robert Cassen. New Brunswick, N.J.: Transactions Publishers.

———, and Robert M. Schmidt. 1996. Toward a cure for the myopia and tunnel vision of the population debate: A dose of historical perspective. In *The impacts of population growth in developing countries*, ed. Dennis Ahlburg, Allen C. Kelley, and Karen Oppenheim Mason. Berlin: Springer-Verlag.

Knack, Stephen, and Philip Keefer. 1995. Institutions and economic performance: Cross-country tests using alternative international measures. *Economics & Politics* 7: 207–27.

Lomborg, Bjørn. 2001. *The skeptical environmentalist*. New York: Cambridge University Press.

Norton, Seth W. 2001. Institutions, population, and human well-being. PERC Working Paper WP01-03. Bozeman, Mont.: PERC.

Panayotou, Theodore. 1994. The population, environment, and development nexus. In *Population and development: Old debates, new conclusions*, ed. Robert Cassen. New Brunswick, N.J.: Transactions Publishers.

Political Risk Services. 1997. *International country risk guide*. East Syracuse, N.Y.: Political Risk Services.

Sachs, Jeffrey D., and Andrew M. Warner. 1997. Fundamental sources of long-run growth. *American Economic Review* 87: 84–188.

Simon, Julian S. 1981. *The ultimate resource*. Princeton, N.J.: Princeton University Press.

———. 1990. *Population matters*. New Brunswick, N.J.: Transaction Publishers.

———. 1995. *The state of humanity*. Oxford: Blackwell.

Solow, Robert M. 1956. A contribution to the theory of economic growth. *Quarterly Journal of Economics* 70: 65–94.

Todaro, Michael P. 1996. *Economic Development*, 6th ed. Reading, Mass.: Addison-Wesley Publishing Company.

United Nations Development Program. 1997. Human development report. New York: Oxford University Press.

World Bank. 2001. World development indicators. CD-ROM. Washington, D.C.: World Bank.

———. Various years. World development indicators. Washington, D.C.: World Bank.

Appendix

Sample Countries

Algeria	Guinea-Bissau	Nigeria
Bangladesh	Haiti	Pakistan
Bhutan	Honduras	Panama
Bolivia	India	Papua New Guinea
Botswana	Indonesia	Paraguay
Burkina Faso	Iran	Peru
Burundi	Iraq	Philippines
Cambodia	Jamaica	Rwanda
Cameroon	Jordan	Senegal
Central African Republic	Kenya	Sierra Leone
Chile	Lao People's	Singapore
China	Democratic Republic	Sri Lanka
Colombia	Lesotho	Sudan
Congo	Libya	Syrian Arab Republic
Costa Rica	Madagascar	Tanzania
Cote d'Ivoire	Malawi	Thailand
Cuba	Mali	Togo
Democratic Republic	Mauritania	Trinidad and Tobago
of Congo	Mauritius	Tunisia
Dominican Repbulic	Mexico	Uganda
Ecuador	Mongolia	United Arab Emirates
Egypt	Morocco	Uruguay
El Salvador	Mozambique	Vietnam
Ethiopia	Myanmar	Yemen
Ghana	Namibia	Zambia
Guatemala	Nicaragua	Zimbabwe
Guinea	Niger	

High and Low Population Growth Countries

High Growth Countries	Low Growth Countries
Botswana	Cambodia [b]
Cote d'Ivoire	Chile [b]
Democratic Republic of Congo [a]	China
Ethiopia [a]	Cuba
Ghana [a]	El Salvador
Honduras [b]	Haiti [b]
Iran [b]	Jamaica
Iraq	Mauritius
Jordan	Mozambique [a]
Kenya	Myanmar [a]
Libya[b]	Sri Lanka
Malawi	Trinidad and Tobago
Syrian Arab Republic [b]	Uruguay
United Arab Emirates	Yemen [a]

[a] Short-term only   [b] Long-term only

High and Low Economic Freedom Countries

High Freedom	Low Freedom
Chile	Algeria
Costa Rica	Bangladesh
Guatamala	Democratic Republic of Congo
Indonesia	Guinea-Bissau
Mauritius	Myanmar
Panama	Nicaragua
Paraguay	Nigeria
Singapore	Sierra Leone
Thailand	Syrian AR
Uruguay	Uganda
Zambia	

Strong and Weak Rule of Law Countries

Strong Law	Weak Law
Botswana	Bangladesh
Chile	Bolivia
China	Colombia
Costa Rica	Democratic Republic of Congo
Cuba	Guatemala
Ecuador	Guinea-Bissau
Namibia	Haiti
Singapore	Iraq
Tanzania	Mauritius
Thailand	Peru
Trinidad and Tobago	Sri Lanka

Variable Descriptions
Measures of Poverty and Environmental Degradation

U.N. Human Poverty Index	An index of human well-being that focuses on human deprivation of survival, education, and knowledge, and economic provisioning (United Nations Development Program 1997)
Death by 40	The proportion of people not expected to survive to age 40 (United Nations Development Program 1997)
Adult illiteracy	The proportion of adults classified as illiterate (United Nations Development Program 1997)
Safe water	Proportion of the population without access to safe water (United Nations Development Program 1997)
Health services	Proportion of the population without access to health services (United Nations Development Program 1997)
Underweight children	Proportion of children under age 5 who are underweight (United Nations Development Program 1997)
Deforestation rate	The average annual permanent conversion of natural forest area to other uses, including shifting cultivation, permanent agriculture, ranching, settlements, and infrastructure development (data are percentage changes) (World Bank, various years)
Water pollution	Organic water pollution (BOD) emissions in kilograms per day per worker (World Bank, various years)
Net savings rate	Gross domestic savings minus consumption of fixed capital (World Bank, various years)
Agricultural productivity	Value added in 1995 U.S. dollars divided by the number of workers in agriculture (World Bank, various years)

Chapter 6

The Relation Between
Net Carbon Emissions
and Income

Robert E. McCormick

ISSUES OF GLOBAL climate change frame one of the most important debates and concerns about the environment today. Unlike most other environmental topics, the issues surrounding global climate change transcend continents and by their very nature seem to defy local, even national governmental solutions. Worse, there is no universal agreement about the problem itself. Serious scholars have data on both sides of the question of global warming, and others have interpreted existing facts in myriad ways. The public seems to believe that the Earth is warming, unnaturally, but public perception, although politically important, is not always scientifically accurate. If all this were not enough, there is even disagreement about the impacts of global climate change, assuming it to be real. One camp is concerned that melting ice and

Robert E. McCormick is professor and BB&T Scholar in the John E. Walker Department of Economics at Clemson University and a senior associate at PERC. This work borrows extensively from joint work coauthored with Joshua Utt and Walker Hunter (Utt, Hunter, and McCormick 2002). Terry Anderson particularly, but also Richard Stroup, Bruce Yandle, and Daniel Benjamin, provided intellectual stimulation and insights that make this work presentable. I acknowledge a debt to all of them and to PERC while retaining residual rights to the effort.

rising sea levels will drown some cities; others claim there is no evidence of global warming; some even say the Earth is cooling. At the same time, some scholars argue that the Earth's warming might be good for humanity—longer growing seasons, more food, and less cold, which kills.[1]

I will not address the question of whether there is or is not unnatural warming of the planet, whether it is good or bad if there is or is not global warming, and whether it is or is not caused by emissions of carbon dioxide or any other gas, solid, or liquid. These questions are interesting and no doubt important, but they are not the focus of this chapter.

Instead I will address several basic issues that appear to be fundamental in context of the debate about global climate change. These include the following:

- What is the correct way to measure carbon and other global warming gas emissions? by country? in total? per capita? per dollar of gross domestic product?

- Do economies that grow and become richer emit more or less than poorer economies?

- Is gross or net gas emissions the correct way to think about global warming?

- How does the United States compare with the rest of the world in carbon gas emissions?

The Complexity of Net Carbon Emissions

There is considerable concern in the environmental movement about the relation between economic activity and what is called global warming.[2] Human economic activity leads to the burning of fossil fuels and plant matter, releasing carbon dioxide. Numerous additional human activities release other gases, such as methane and chlorofluorocarbon compounds. In turn, increases in carbon dioxide, methane, and other carbon compounds in the atmosphere are argued to cause the Earth to retain additional heat from the sun and thus warm in an unnatural way. This has led to many proposals to control the emissions of greenhouse gases, notably the Kyoto Protocol.

Even though the protocol sometimes recognizes that net emissions, not gross emissions, are the relevant concern, popular discussion and great chunks of academic discourse seem blindly focused on gross emissions. Little attention is paid to the substantial chunks of carbon sequestered in trees and forests, farms, crops and groundcover, buildings, furniture, clothes, landfills, and other organic possessions.

The net amount of carbon in the atmosphere depends on the difference between the amount of carbon sequestered in sinks and the amount emitted by sources. The terrestrial stock of carbon is increased by the growth of carbon sinks. A sink is an object, like a tree (or group of objects, like a forest), in the terrestrial sphere that stores more carbon in a given year than it emits. The terrestrial stock of carbon is decreased and the atmospheric stock increased by burning carbon sources such as fossil fuels, usually done to create energy. A source is an object or activity in the terrestrial sphere that emits more carbon into the atmosphere than it stores. So a growing forest would tend to be a sink, and a forest fire would tend to be a source.

Many carbon stocks vary from year to year as either a sink or source. For instance, landfills, although growing in volume and hence storing carbon, also emit methane to the atmosphere. Careful study is required to determine whether they are a source or sink in a given year. Similarly, growing trees add to the stock of solid carbon or increase the stock of gaseous carbon depending on their growth and decay rates.

As an example, carbon may be sequestered by trees and deposited into landfills. The initial sequestration occurs in a given year, either as increased tree volume or wood production. The transfer of carbon to the landfill is merely a location change in stored carbon and, as such, is not sequestration but rather a movement of storage location.

Carbon sequestration is the process whereby gaseous carbon is removed from the atmosphere and stored in the terrestrial sphere.

Sequestrations can take place either as deliberate human practices, such as removing carbon dioxide from the air and cooling it for transport to some place for some other purpose (dry ice is an example) or as the result of natural processes or human-induced activities with unintended consequences. The warming of dry ice would, for example, return the carbon to the atmosphere as gas.

Oceans

The chemistry of carbon states is complex and controversial, but there are a number of agreed-upon principles. For instance, the ocean holds about fifty times more carbon than the atmosphere in the form of dissolved inorganic and organic carbon (Intergovernmental Panel on Climate Change 2000, 1.2.1.2, 31). In the ocean, carbon is sequestered by plantlike phytoplankton, which in turn is consumed by sea animals. Some of this carbon rains down toward the ocean floor as waste and dead organisms. Bacteria feed on this particulate organic carbon and produce carbon dioxide, which dissolves in the water. The rest of the detritus ends up on the sea floor (Preuss 2001).

Evidence suggests that the ocean removes three times more carbon—and holds nineteen times more in storage (U.S. Department of Energy 1999)—from the atmosphere per year than the terrestrial system. Carbon also cycles between land and ocean. The ocean gains carbon in the form of runoff from the terrestrial system, and carbon is removed from the oceanic reservoir through the process of sedimentation of organic remains and inorganic carbonate shell material. However, it is the variability in carbon flux between the atmosphere and land that primarily explains the annual variability in atmospheric carbon.[3] In other words, although the store of carbon and the annual flux of carbon are both greater for the ocean than the terrestrial system, most of the atmospheric variability over time is because of flux from or to land.[4]

Fossil Fuels

Carbon cycles from the terrestrial sphere to the atmosphere primarily when fossil fuels storing carbon are used in energy production. Some of the fossil fuels used for energy include petroleum, coal, and natural gas. Consider the United States, the main focus of this research. Between 1950 and 1970, U.S. energy consumption per person rose from 229 million to 334 million BTUs. Between 1970 and 1999, the change was much less drastic, with a consumption of 354 million BTUs per person in 1999. Between 1949 and 1999, energy consumption per dollar of gross domestic product (GDP) fell by half, from 20.63 thousand to 10.92 thousand BTUs per (1996) dollar of GDP (U.S. Department of Energy 2001, Table 1.5, 13). Energy use itself has also become more efficient with respect to carbon emissions. Over the century, natural gas has replaced coal in industrial, commercial, and residential energy use to become the second-biggest energy source, behind petroleum. In 1999, natural gas use produced 1.32 pounds of carbon dioxide per kilowatt-hour, whereas coal produced 2.09 pounds (U.S. Department of Energy and U.S. Environmental Protection Agency 2000).

Agriculture

Energy consumption is a primary source of airborne carbon emissions, but there are other sources that emit carbon naturally via methane, including livestock, rice paddies, and wetlands. Livestock include cattle (dairy and beef), swine, poultry, and others, but cattle alone are responsible for more than 90 percent of methane produced by enteric fermentation, a process in which microbes residing in animal digestive systems break down the feed consumed by the animal. Enteric fermentation accounted for 19 percent of all methane produced by the United States in 1998, exceeded only by the amount produced in landfills (U.S. Environmental Protection Agency 2000). Between 1927 and 2000, the number of milk-producing cattle dropped by more than half, from 21.4 million to 9.2 million. During that same time, milk production nearly doubled, from 89 billion to 167 billion pounds because of the fourfold increase in productivity of the cattle (U.S. Department of Agriculture 2001). In order to understand correctly how enteric fermentation has changed because of increased production technology, further research must be done to determine how the larger quantities of feed necessary to provide higher milk production have increased emissions per animal.

Although cattle and other livestock are a source of carbon and methane emissions, these animals also stand to be significant sources of carbon sinks via the carbon stored in their bodies. Raising livestock reduces the amount of airborne carbon. The emissions have to be compared with the sequestrations.

Livestock plays another role in methane emissions. The decomposition of organic animal waste (manure) in an anaerobic environment produces methane, but the amount of methane produced depends on the style of manure treatment or management. Liquid systems tend to encourage anaerobic conditions and produce significant quantities of methane, whereas solid waste management produces little or no methane. Between 1990 and 1998, emissions from this source increased by 53 percent because of the swine and dairy industries' shift toward larger facilities, which tend to use liquid management systems.

A main focus of this research agenda is to expand on the link between income and carbon emissions. In this regard, the relationship between agricultural and overall economic activity stand to be important. For example, the planting of trees is affected by changes in income and stages of economic growth. During the first part of the twentieth century, the number of U.S. farms was increasing. Between 1910 and 1935, the number of farms grew by 6 percent, before the beginning of a steady decline that persisted into the 1990s (U.S. Department of Agriculture 2001). In 1950, 1.202 billion acres of the United States were used as farmland. The area used for farming increased to a high of 1.205 billion acres in 1955, then decreased steadily until today. In

1999, only 947.44 million acres of land were used for farming. A large portion of U.S. farmland was built on previously forested lands, and many of these abandoned farms reverted back to forest. Between 1982 and 1997, 1,108,400 net acres of prime farmland (considered prime farmland in 1982) were converted to forest (U.S. Department of Agriculture, National Resource Conservation Service 2000). During the same time period, land areas with biomass containing the lowest carbon content, pastureland and rangeland, were reduced (U.S. Department of Agriculture, National Resource Conservation Service 2000).

Wetlands

Wetlands are most likely the largest natural source of methane emissions into the atmosphere. Methanogenic bacteria found in wetlands produce methane through anaerobic decomposition of organic materials. Between 1986 and 1997, a net of 644,000 acres of wetlands were drained. The Fish and Wildlife Service reported to Congress that the estimated wetland loss rate in 1997 was 58,500 acres annually (U.S. Fish and Wildlife Service 2001). Although the environmental benefit of preserving wetlands is left for other studies, draining wetlands may reduce the annual amount of methane produced (Augenbran, Matthews, and Sarma 1997).

Forests

The level of atmospheric carbon decreases when terrestrial stocks of carbon grow over time. The primary terrestrial sinks are forest and soil. The forest ecosystem stores carbon in four major forms: trees, soils, understory, and the floor. "Trees" includes all above- and below-ground portions of all live and dead trees. This includes the merchantable stem, limbs, tops, cull sections, stump, foliage, bark and root bark, and coarse tree roots. "Soils" includes all organic carbon in mineral horizons to a depth of one meter, excluding coarse tree roots. "Understory" includes all live vegetation except trees. "Floor" includes all dead organic matter above the mineral soil horizons except standing dead trees: litter, humus, other woody debris, and so on.

Many variables affect the forest carbon stock. Forest tree volume increases as a result of new plantings or growth in existing trees. Forest tree volume declines as a result of harvesting or burning. Several variables affect the growth of trees, including age, weather, fire suppression, and understory biomass. When old growth forests are allowed to grow for long periods, carbon flux declines to essentially zero. Fire suppression, beginning after the 1930s, has had a large impact on carbon sequestration. Between 1919 and 1929, more than twenty-six million acres of wild land burned on average each year. During the next decade, almost forty million acres burned each year. As a result of enormous expenditures on fire suppression, the average annual burn area between 1990 and 1999 was 3,647,597 acres, a reduction of more than 90 percent (National Interagency Fire Center 2001). Between 1994 and 2000, U.S. federal agencies spent $4,334,840,600 on fire suppression. Fire suppression, and its resulting addition to carbon sequestration, would seem to be positively influenced by the growth in U.S. income.[5]

Another factor affecting carbon sequestration is the rate of harvest of existing forests. The rate of harvest is influenced by the demand for wood used for fuel or wood products. Harvested wood no longer accumulates carbon; however, it can act as storage for differing periods of time. Wood harvested for fuel acts as carbon storage until the wood is burned and the carbon is released. Wood harvested for wood or paper products may exist as carbon storage indefinitely as treated or sealed wood may decay at a very slow rate.

Wood harvesting and clear-cutting for agriculture grew as the United States was settled in the eighteenth century. As wood fuel was replaced with fossil fuels midway through the nineteenth century, harvest rates slowed in many regions and wood for fuel consumption nearly disappeared, only to reemerge during the Depression and the oil shocks of the 1970s. By the 1950s and 1960s, many forest regions began to accumulate carbon faster than it was harvested, resulting in overall carbon sequestration. Between 1976 and 1996, harvest rates remained constant in the Northeast and fell dramatically in the Pacific Northwest and Rocky Mountains. On the other hand, a resurgence in fuel wood use and increasingly intensive use of forests for wood products caused harvest rates in the South (already the highest in 1976) to increase by more than 50 percent.[6] The net effect was a 12 percent national increase in removal of forest between 1976 and 1996. This is independent of the flux in the forest carbon stock attributable to tree growth.

Technology in wood harvesting also affects carbon sequestration. The efficiency of industrial wood harvesting improved over time, so that more wood was removed per hectare and less left as slash (dead vegetation). Whether this affects carbon sequestration positively or negatively depends on the end use of the harvested wood. If the harvested wood is being used to produce wood products, the slash will decay at a relatively faster rate than those products. If the harvested wood is to be burned for energy, the slash will store carbon for a longer period than the harvested wood. And because the majority of wood is used for products rather than fuel, especially in richer economies, the reduction in slash over time has had a positive impact on carbon sequestration.

Another important carbon sink that has been growing over time is woody biomass outside of forests. Savanna ecosystems are composed of two major competing types of biomass: grassland formations and woody plants. Woody plants include shrub-steppe, desert scrub, wood land, or forest. Over the past century, woody plants have occupied an increasing percentage of land. In the United States, this woody encroachment stores most of the carbon contained in nonforest, non-cropland biomass. Many theories have been proposed as to the growing encroachment, including fire suppression, overgrazing, and nitrogen deposition. The annual burn area of the United States has declined by 95 percent since 1850, significantly reducing one source of carbon emissions (Pacala et al. 2001). As a result, woody plants, which historically were burned, are covering a much larger area. Changes in soils and microclimate accompanying long-term heavy grazing may have shifted the balance more to woody plants better adapted to nutrient-poor soils (Archer, Boutton, and Hibbard 2000). This growth previously was unaccounted for in studies of the U.S. carbon budget.

Soil

Soil organic carbon makes up about two-thirds of the carbon pool in the terrestrial biosphere (Allmaras et al. 2000). This carbon is in the form of plant, animal, and microbial residues in all stages of decomposition. By contrast, the only significant vegetation that stores carbon is located in forest biomass and woody plants. Soils, on the other hand, store carbon regardless of local vegetation (Intergovernmental Panel on Climate Change 2000, 1.2.1.2). Temperate and tropical forests (not located in the United States) store more carbon in the local vegetation than the local soil. However, biomass in most other areas contains less carbon than the corresponding soil. Hence there is more carbon stored nationally in soil than in vegetation. It is therefore important that a study of carbon sequestration account for soil-bound carbon in addition to carbon stored in biomass.

Carbon Emissions

Total emissions of carbon dioxide in the United States from all sources for the years 1900–1999 in carbon equivalents are plotted in Figure 6.1,[7] which reveals that carbon emissions have been on the increase, basically without interruption, for the entire past century.[8]

Figure 6.2 corrects total emissions for changes in population and reports emissions per capita for the past century.[9] Emissions per capita in the United States, while growing some in the first half of the twentieth century (most of the growth occurring in the first twenty years of the century), have been flat or declining for the past quarter-century.

Figure 6.3 plots the emissions per capita in the United States versus

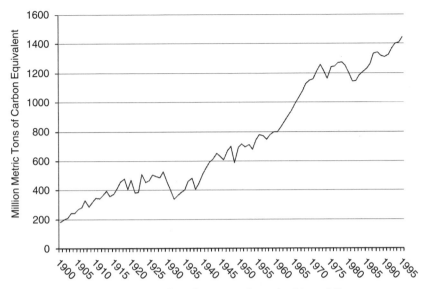

Figure 6.1   Total Emissions of Carbon Dioxide in the United States,
1900–1999
Source: Marland, Boden, and Andres (2002)

income for the period of 1929 through 1996.[10] Emissions rise with real
income, up to about $5,000 per person per year; thereafter, they are
relatively flat. As Figures 6.2 and 6.3 reveal, emissions per capita are
not currently on the rise in the United States, that is, not over the past
twenty-five years.[11] Combining this fact with the observation that total
emissions are on the rise means population growth or exporting activities
account for all of the rise in carbon dioxide emissions in the United
States over the past quarter century, and the greatest portion of the
growth in emissions for the entire past one hundred years. This suggests
that policies directed toward lowering carbon dioxide emissions should
take extra care, because the issue is population growth, not growth in
carbon emissions per person.

Another way to analyze carbon emissions is to compute emissions
per dollar of GDP. This, in a way, measures how efficiently an economy
uses its energy to create output. Carbon emissions per dollar of real

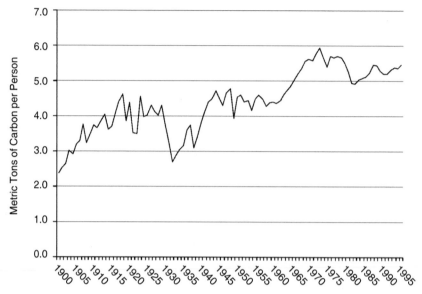

Figure 6.2   Total Carbon Emissions per Person in the United States,
1900–1999
Source: Marland, Boden, and Andres (2002)

GDP have been on the decline, almost continuously, for the past half
century in the United States. Figure 6.4 plots the U.S. energy consumption per dollar of GDP (1996 terms). This steady decrease is due
to increasing energy efficiency in the production of its national consumption and to the switch from manufacturing to services in national
production.[12]

Visual examination of the data charted in Figure 6.4 suggests and
statistical analysis confirms a prediction of declining emissions per
capita once the income level is sufficiently high.[13] U.S. GDP per person
is now in the low $30,000-per-person range, which is near the critical
value where emissions per capita should start to decline.[14] Hence, per-
capita carbon emissions can be expected to decline if economic growth
continues.

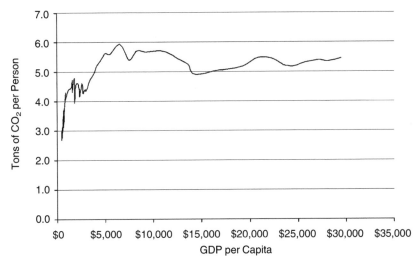

Figure 6.3   Gross Carbon Emissions per Person and Income in the
United States, 1929–1996
Source: U.S. Department of Commerce, Bureau of Economic Affairs 2002

Carbon Sequestration

Just as income affects carbon emissions, it affects carbon sequestration.
Consider carbon sequestered in U.S. forests, for example. As a result
of increased forest acreage, total carbon sequestration in forests was up
about 47 percent between 1952 and 2000 (see Figure 6.5).[15] Annual
forest sequestration per capita was nearly constant from 1960 to 1970,
increased sharply through 1980, but decreased thereafter (see Figure
6.6).

Standard statistical modeling techniques show that national forest
acreage grows with income, but at a decreasing rate. Acreage per person
is a function of real GDP and the relationship is positive, but somewhat
complex. Income and forest acreage are positively linked, and carbon
sequestrations grow with income. Thus, there is evidence that income
and carbon sequestrations, via forests, are positively linked. This evi-

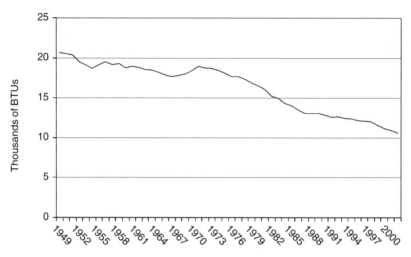

Figure 6.4   U.S. Energy Consumption Corrected for GDP
Note: In terms of 1996 dollars
Source: U.S. Department of Energy, Energy Information Administration 2002

dence is good news for those who fear global warming. Higher incomes are linked with larger amounts of earthbound carbon sequestrations.

There are other sources of sequestration besides trees. As agriculture has become more productive, the amount of cropland in temperate regions has fallen, and agricultural practices are the most important variable in the accumulation of soil organic carbon. In 1997, 25 percent of the 1.5 billion acres of U.S. nonfederal land were considered cropland. The conversion of natural vegetation to cultivated use inevitably leads to an immediate loss of carbon in soil. Some estimates suggest that cultivated croplands in the United States lose about 2.7 terragrams of carbon per year (Gebhart et al. 1994). This loss in carbon can be attributed to reduced inputs of organic matter, increased decomposability of crop residues, and tillage effects that decrease the amount of physical protection to decomposition (Post and Kwon 2000). Tillage-induced changes of perennial grasses to annual crop species reduce root biomass and inputs of carbon from roots to soils. Fluxes in carbon

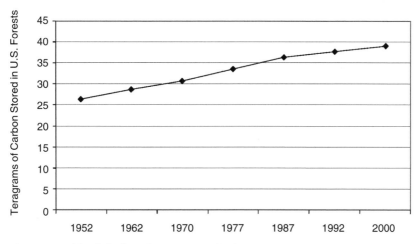

Figure 6.5   Total Carbon Storage in U.S. Forests
Source: Birdsey and Heath (1995)

are therefore tied to the area of land that is taken in and out of agriculture each year, as well as to the technology of agriculture used on existing croplands.

Because the acreage of total U.S. farmland has declined over most of the past century and because cropland is typically a net source of carbon emissions, abandoning cropland stands to reduce net emissions irrespective of whether the land reverts to forest or other significant biomass. In fact, the U.S. Conservation Reserve Program, established to reduce water and wind erosion on more than 45 million acres of erodible and environmentally sensitive cropland, restored 21 percent of soil organic carbon lost during tillage in just five years. Cropland treated this way has the potential to sequester 45 percent of the 38.1 terragrams of carbon emitted annually into the atmosphere by U.S. agriculture (Gebhart et al. 1994).

Lower tillage intensity (less mixing and stirring of the soil) has also decreased net carbon emissions from agriculture. As incomes rise and technology develops, agriculture has naturally moved toward a system

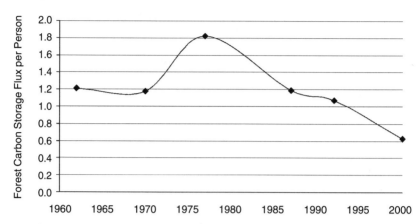

Figure 6.6   Annual Forest Carbon Sequestration per Person in the
United States
Note: The vertical scale is in metric tons of carbon flux per million people.
Source: Birdsey and Heath (1995)

that favors fewer net carbon emissions from soil use (see Post and Kwon
2000).

The atmospheric stock of carbon also decreases when the carbon
stock in anthropogenic sinks grows. Such sinks include landfills, buildings, manufactured agricultural products, automobiles, manufactured
wood products, and living bodies. Wood and agricultural products store
a significant amount of carbon for varying amounts of time, depending
on end use.

Approximately 16 percent of all discarded municipal solid waste is
incinerated. The remainder is disposed of in landfills. Forty-one percent
of U.S. landfill volume is taken up by paper and paperboard, 7.9 percent
is food waste, and 17.9 percent is yard waste (Micales and Skog 1998).
Therefore the majority of cellulose and hemicellulose in landfills origi-
nates from forest and agricultural products. This represents a large
amount of carbon being sequestered each year. The U.S. Forest Service
has estimated that none to 3 percent of the carbon from wood and an
average of 26 percent of the carbon from paper is potentially released

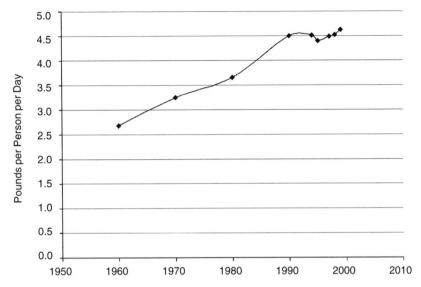

Figure 6.7   U.S. Landfill Storage per Person per Day over Time
Source: U.S. Environmental Protection Agency (2001)

into the atmosphere as carbon dioxide and methane once the material has been put into landfills (Micales and Skog 1998). Moreover, the percentage susceptible to release has fallen over time as waste has been deposited in landfills that seal the waste and limit the amount of decay from oxygen. Though this slows the decay rate of wood products and increases stored carbon, it produces more methane relative to carbon dioxide. Because methane has a greater impact on global warming potential, the flux in net carbon emissions must be weighted by this effect.

The portion of garbage recovered or recycled is increasing, but this increase is dominated by the increase in the total amount of garbage created. The United States is increasingly creating garbage and disposing of it as landfill. The stock of carbon being buried, assuming a constant fraction of garbage is carbon, is rising. Landfills are a carbon sink, depending upon the amount of methane released. Figure 6.7

reveals that Americans are increasingly accumulating resources in land-fills, although at what appears to be a decreasing rate.

The amount of carbon stored in buildings, automobiles, animals, and persons is a function mainly of the growth in the total number of those goods and organisms over time. Because the flux is positive for many or all of these categories, a reasonable assumption is that carbon storage has risen accordingly.

For example, animal and human populations have been growing in size so that they can meaningfully affect net terrestrial carbon. The growth in the size and weight of human population embodied more carbon in the past century. This carbon flux ranges from 0.025 million metric tons of sequestration in 1901 to 0.042 million metric tons in 1991. The numbers are small relative to overall emissions, but the intuition is correct: Human population growth has contributed slightly to carbon sequestration in the form of living matter. The carbon flux attributable to growth in the stock of cattle is similar. Between 1921 and 1999, the average annual carbon flux attributable to the growth in the stock of cattle is 0.045 million metric tons of carbon per year.[16] The average sequestration attributable to hogs is much smaller, equivalent to 0.004 million metric tons of carbon per year.[17] Additional analysis of animal carbon stores follows later in this chapter.

There is also carbon transfer between land and the land-based aquatic system that occurs within terrestrial waterways, such as reservoirs and rivers. Although the total carbon storage in the terrestrial aquatic system (lakes, rivers, reservoirs, and so on) is small relative to that of forests and soil, its growth rate in carbon storage is significant enough that it may account for more than 5 percent of the carbon sequestered within the United States between 1980 and 1990 (Pacala et al. 2001). Rivers also export a small quantity of sequestered carbon to the sea. By some estimates, the total export of dissolved inorganic carbon and particulate organic carbon to the sea may account for another 5 percent of U.S. carbon sequestration.

Net Emissions

The primary point is that carbon naturally and unnaturally fluxes and flows between solid and gaseous states. But how does human economic activity influence the rate of flux and the stores of carbon in each of these two states? On the one hand, carbon emissions grow with income—richer economies consume more carbon energy sources—but carbon storage in the terrestrial sphere probably grows as well as richer people accumulate wealth in the form of material things, many of which are carbon-based. The question thus becomes: Which grows faster as incomes increase, emissions or sequestrations? Do the causes and effects of the income growth when the economy is relatively poor—dirty energy consumption, growth in agriculture, and deforestation—spur a net surplus of sources over sinks? Does economic growth when the country is relatively richer—the shift to service industries, afforestation, and less dirty energy use—lead to a decrease in the disparity or perhaps a net surplus of sinks over sources? According to so-called environmental Kuznets curve literature (see Chapter 3 of this book), pollution increases with industrial and income growth until some turning point. After this inflection, additional income growth leads to enhanced environmental quality.

International treaties such as the Kyoto Protocol propose to set caps on carbon emissions in order to limit the growth of atmospheric carbon. Because this will almost surely reduce energy production in the short term, this could cause a contraction in national income. At a minimum, the growth rate of income will slow. If it is true that net carbon emissions rise and fall with income, this policy might have the perverse effect of keeping a country at an income level at which carbon sources are greater than carbon sinks. In the end, a cap on emissions might actually increase the amount of airborne carbon. And to those worried about global warming, this might make the world warmer.

Several statistics point to the possibility that economic growth in the United States may lead to a decrease in net carbon emissions. First, carbon emissions from energy production by developed and transition economies fell from the 1980s to the 1990s. During the same time period, emissions increased by more than 50 percent for low-income nations. Second, emissions from the second largest source, land-use change such as conversion of forests to cropland, diminished from the 1980s to the 1990s (Intergovernmental Panel on Climate Change 1990).

Table 6.1 lists total emissions and sequestrations as computed in this study for the United States over the period 1962 through 1998, and Figure 6.8 plots net emissions per capita. The chart suggests that net emissions were rising until the early 1970s, fell until the early 1980s, and have been rising since. This pattern follows intuition about the link between net emissions and income. The 1970s experienced slow or even negative growth in the United States, whereas growth and economic activity picked up in the 1980s and into the 1990s.

Figure 6.9 plots net emissions per real GDP per capita. Statistical analysis of these data are only suggestive. On the one hand, total net emissions seem to be negatively linked with GDP (higher GDP reduces total net emissions). At the same time, net emissions per person are either flat or rising. The exact statistical relationships are complex so a clear picture does not emerge. However, it is certainly the case that the growth of total net emissions has slowed, and detailed statistical analysis suggests that total net emissions of carbon will start falling when income exceeds about $35,000 per person in 1996 terms.[18] This is just above the current level of income per capita in the United States today. This analysis suggests that the United States is nearing the apex of the environmental Kuznets curve for net carbon emissions. All told, these data suggest additional economic growth should bring declining net emissions of airborne carbon per person within the United States. The United States appears on the road to being a net carbon sink and this is in spite of its great use of energy and large level of emissions. The data say that rich people consume—but they also accumulate.

Table 6.1
U.S. Emissions and Sequestrations of Carbon

	Total Emissions	Total Sequestrations	Net Emissions	Net Emissions per Capita
1962	828.582	426.1	402.5	0.219974
1963	872.512	441.6	430.9	0.231992
1964	909.595	438.7	470.9	0.249881
1965	944.815	454.8	490.0	0.256451
1966	996.098	462.1	534.0	0.276011
1967	1035.509	478.8	556.7	0.284742
1968	1077.381	476.8	600.5	0.304260
1969	1128.385	480.6	647.8	0.325011
1970	1152.145	470.1	682.1	0.335498
1971	1159.217	530.7	628.6	0.303907
1972	1211.838	553.7	658.1	0.314468
1973	1259.274	591.8	667.5	0.315820
1974	1214.83	594.5	620.3	0.290774
1975	1164.477	636.0	528.5	0.245266
1976	1244.362	671.9	572.4	0.263110
1977	1248.602	709.5	539.1	0.245327
1978	1281.887	711.3	570.6	0.256920
1979	1292.801	724.9	567.9	0.252872
1980	1262.782	696.8	566.0	0.249843
1981	1217.507	718.8	498.7	0.217334
1982	1156.118	707.9	448.2	0.193487
1983	1159.142	620.8	538.4	0.230280
1984	1203.247	681.6	521.6	0.221197
1985	1215.008	685.3	529.7	0.222624
1986	1216.079	653.6	562.5	0.234254
1987	1259.909	624.9	635.0	0.262088
1988	1328.802	583.7	745.1	0.304760
1989	1337.681	626.7	711.0	0.288055
1990	1314.394	636.7	677.7	0.271671
1991	1321.685	616.6	705.0	0.279610
1992	1327.371	657.7	669.7	0.262601
1993	1388.431	591.8	796.6	0.309019
1994	1419.436	643.8	775.6	0.297945
1995	1417.295	580.1	837.2	0.318551
1996	1456.189	603.8	852.4	0.321375
1997	1484.944	600.3	884.6	0.330343
1998	1486.801	590.6	896.2	0.331626

Note: See Utt, Hunter, and McCormick (2002) for details on computational methods.

Figure 6.8   Net Carbon Emissions per Person in the United States
Source: See Utt, Hunter, and McCormick (2002, 43–47) for computations and technique.

International Comparisons

The United States is often characterized as the world's greatest polluter, and in the context of global climate change, the United States is regularly seen by the world as dragging its feet on dealing with the question of global warming, carbon emissions, and climate change. This section reports some data for international comparisons.

Data on gross carbon emissions are available for most countries for a long time span.[19] Figure 6.10 uses these data to plot the annual emissions of carbon dioxide per person for the world for the period 1950 through 1996, and the results are profound. Gross or total global carbon emissions per capita are essentially constant over the past thirty years. And, as previously discussed, they have actually declined in the United States over this period. Although total emissions have grown, again, the

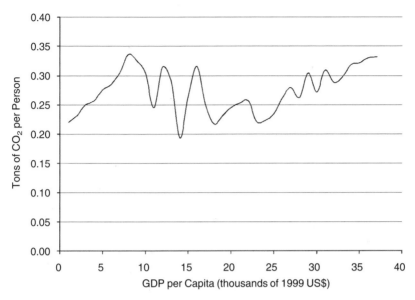

Figure 6.9 Net Carbon Emissions per Real GDP per Person, 1962–1998
Source: Utt, Hunter, and McCormick (2002, 47)

problem is not with individual carbon emissions per se, but with the fact that there are more people.

Putting all these pieces together, given the fact that global gross emissions of carbon per capita are at worse flat, but are quite probably decreasing, global warming, if it is a social problem, is a problem of population growth, not of wealthy individuals and growing economies. Quite the opposite is true. If there is a policy prescription, it is that we should pursue policies that spur economic growth and wealth accumulation. Less net carbon emissions will follow.

It is also noteworthy that the fertility rates seem to decline with income (see Becker and Barro 1988; Chapter 5 of this book). Thus richer societies also procreate at a slower rate. However, richer people tend to be healthier and longer-lived. Hence, the relation between carbon emissions, population, and income begs further study.

The United States is often portrayed as the world's greatest polluter

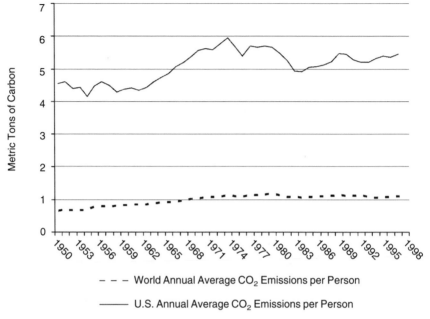

− − − World Annual Average CO_2 Emissions per Person

——— U.S. Annual Average CO_2 Emissions per Person

Figure 6.10   World Annual Emissions of Carbon Dioxide per Person
Source: Carbon Dioxide Information Analysis Center 2002

because its gross emissions per capita are more than four times the world average. Figure 6.11, however, tells a slightly different story. The ratio of U.S. gross emissions relative to the world is declining. As a member of the world, the United States is emitting a smaller and smaller portion of the gross carbon emissions into the atmosphere on a per-capita basis. Whatever else might be true, neither U.S. nor world carbon gas emissions are growing on a per-person basis. Moreover, relative to the rest of the world, the United States is emitting less and less per person.

Closing Thoughts

Do increases in economic activity lead an economy to take carbon out of the air? There is certainly reason for hope that the answer to this

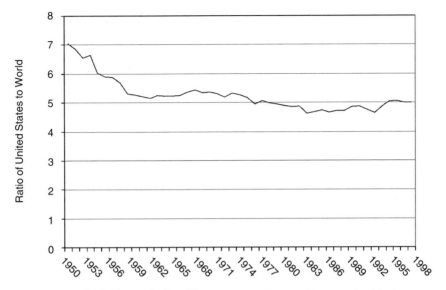

Figure 6.11   U.S. Gross Carbon Emissions per Person Compared with the Rest of the World
Source: Carbon Dioxide Information Analysis Center 2002

question is yes. Based on direct evidence from the United States coupled with indirect evidence from the rest of the world, it does appear that richer economies take more carbon out of the air than poorer ones. Hence, a unidimensional focus on carbon emissions—looking only at what comes out of the tailpipes of automobiles, for example—stands to result in errors in analysis and policy. Results presented in this chapter bolster the argument that richer people also suck substantial amounts of carbon out of the air into animals, trees, landfills, buildings, and other material possessions. Statistical analysis in this chapter forecasts that the growth rate of net carbon emissions per person will soon be negative in the United States, as long as income continues to grow. If that trend continues—and there is every reason to believe that it will—the United States is likely to become a carbon sink. Based on this evidence, the Kyoto Protocol and other regulations on economic activity may do more harm than good. Regulators of carbon emissions should take great care not to kill the goose that lays the golden eggs. The results presented in this chapter indicate that net carbon emissions will decline if economies grow and people get richer. The analysis supports the view that higher incomes are associated with a better natural environment. Fascination with emissions controls and the Kyoto Protocol is somewhat hard to understand in this context.

One simple but profound fact remains. Even while U.S. and global total gross emissions are on the rise, there is little or no growth in total or gross carbon emissions per person in either the United States or the world. Moreover, taking sequestrations into account, there is even less of an issue with carbon emissions.

Notes

1. There are many places where one might go to investigate these contentions in detail. A sampler includes http://www.pewclimate.org; http://www.globalchange.org; http://www.epa.gov/globalwarming; http://www.ipcc.ch; http://gcmd.gsfc.nasa.gov; http://www.co2science.org; and Julian Simon (1995, 1999).

2. Again, let me emphasize that I borrow heavily here from earlier, joint work with Utt and Hunter (see Utt, Hunter, and McCormick 2002).

3. Intergovernmental Panel on Climate Change (2000, 1.2.1.3, 32) lists five sources in support of this contention.

4. The rate of carbon uptake is limited by the solubility of carbon dioxide in seawater and by the slow transfer between the surface and deep waters (Intergovernmental Panel on Climate Change 2000, 1.2.1.3, 32). The limited solubility of carbon dioxide can be pictured by considering how quickly a carbonated beverage goes flat after being exposed to air. Carbon is stored more effectively at greater depths; however, carbon cycles very slowly within the ocean. Waters circulate between surface and deep layers on varying time scales from 250 years in the Atlantic Ocean to 1,000 years for parts of the Pacific Ocean (U.S. Department of Energy 1999).

5. Technological advances in silviculture have likely promoted additional carbon sequestration over time. Because the technology and science of silviculture are positively affected by economic growth, it is reasonable to assert that income growth is linked to carbon sequestration on these grounds as well.

6. Data provided by Brad Smith, Forest Inventory and Analysis, U.S. Forest Service.

7. A carbon equivalent measures the amount of carbon in a compound. For instance, the atomic weight of carbon dioxide is 44, of which carbon is 12. Therefore, a ton of carbon equivalent carbon dioxide actually weighs 3.6667 tons. Put differently, 3.6667 tons of carbon dioxide contain one ton of carbon.

8. There are two exceptions, the early 1930s and the early 1980s. The first is likely traced to the Depression. The second is more mysterious.

9. Remember that carbon dioxide, although by far the largest component of total carbon emissions into the atmosphere, is not the only one. There is, for instance, methane. Moreover, in the context of the normative problem of global warming, there are noncarbon compounds that most scientists claim also warm the climate. These include, for instance, nitrous and nitric oxides. Worse yet, again in the context of the normative analysis of global warming, not all carbon molecules act the same. Many scientists argue, for instance, that carbon in methane has twenty-one times the global warming potential of carbon in carbon dioxide. Carbon in certain chlorofluorocarbon compounds has, by some estimates, 11,000 times the potential. Hence, in the analysis presented here some caution is in order, for only emissions of carbon in carbon dioxide are being measured. Other sources, a relatively small portion of the global warming situation, are omitted here.

10. This period was chosen because of data limitation on GDP for the United States.

11. This visual conclusion is supported in the statistical analysis as well. The full results are reported in Utt, Hunter, and McCormick (2002).

12. Without doubt a great deal of additional investigation is warranted here. Specifically, a cross-sectional analysis seems appropriate to disentangle the impact of changing income from the changing structure of output, and whether or how these latter two effects are related.

13. See Utt, Hunter, and McCormick (2002) for more details.

14. See Utt, Hunter, and McCormick (2002) for the details.

15. These data are not measured each year, but sporadically within the time frame: 1952, 1962, 1970, 1977, 1987, 1992, and 2000.

16. This excludes methane emissions emanating from cattle, but those emissions are already included in alternate versions of the U.S. carbon budget. What is generally left out of the budget is the flux attributable to the growth in stock.

17. What this discussion leaves out is the long-term fate of human and animal carbon. Some forms of this carbon are stored long-term in various forms, whether as products or as matter in landfills or graves. This long-term sequestration has not been accounted for in previous studies.

18. Again, the detail of methods and computations can be found in Utt, Hunter, and McCormick (2002).

19. See Carbon Dioxide Information Analysis Center, "National Fossil-Fuel CO2 Emissions," at http://cdiac.esd.ornl.gov/trends/emis/tre_coun.htm.

References

Allmaras, Raymond R., Harry H. Schomberg, Clyde L. Douglas Jr., and Thanh H. Dao. 2000. Soil organic carbon sequestration potential of adopting conservation tillage in U.S. croplands. *Journal of Soil and Water Conservation* 55 (3): 365–73.

Archer, Steven R., Thoms W. Boutton, and Kathy A. Hibbard. 2000. Trees in grasslands: Biogeochemical consequences of woody plant expansion. In *Global biogeochemical cycles in the climate system*, ed. E. D. Schulze, S. P. Harrison, M. Heimann, E. A. Holland, J. Lloyd, I. C. Prentice, and D. Schimel. San Diego, Calif.: Academic Press, 115–37.

Augenbran, Harvey, Elaine Matthews, and David Sarma. 1997. *The global methane cycle*. New York: Institute on Climate and Planets, U.S. National Aeronautics and Space Administration. Online: http://icp.giss.nasa.gov/research/methane/gmc.html.

Becker, Gary S., and Robert J. Barro. 1988. A reformulation of the economic theory of fertility. *Quarterly Journal of Economics* 103 (February 1): 1–25.

Birdsey, Richard A., and Linda S. Heath. 1995. Carbon changes in U.S. forests. In *Productivity of America's forests and climate change*, ed. Linda A. Joyce. Fort Collins, Colo.: USDA Forest Service, 56–70.

Carbon Dioxide Information Analysis Center. National fossil-fuel CO_2 emissions. Online: http://cdiac.esd.ornl.gov/trends/emis/tre_coun.htm.

Gebhart, Dick L., Hyrum B. Johnson, H. S. Mayeux, and H. W. Polley. 1994. The CRP increases soil organic carbon. *Journal of Soil and Water Conservation* 49 (5): 488–92.

Intergovernmental Panel on Climate Change (IPCC). 1990. *Climate change—the IPCC scientific assessment*, ed. John T. Houghton, G. J. Jenkins, and J. J. Ephraums. Cambridge, Mass.: Cambridge University Press.

————. 2000. *Special report on land use, land-use change, and forestry*, ed.

Robert T. Watson, Ian R. Noble, Bert Bolin, N. H. Ravindranath, David J. Verardo, and David J. Dokken. Cambridge, Mass.: Cambridge University Press.

Marland, G., T. A. Boden, and R. J. Andres. 2002. Global, regional, and national CO_2 emissions. In *Trends: A compendium of data on global change*. Oak Ridge, Tenn.: Carbon Dioxide Information Analysis Center, Oak Ridge National Laboratory, U.S. Department of Energy. Online: http://cdiac .esd.ornl.gov/trends/emis/tre_coun.htm.

Micales, Jessie A., and Kenneth E. Skog. 1998. The decomposition of forest products in landfills. *International Biodeterioration & Biodegradation* 39 (July/August): 145–58.

National Interagency Fire Center. 2001. Wildland fire statistics. Online: http://www.nifc.gov/stats/wildlandfirestats.html.

Norton, Seth W. 2004. Population Growth, Economic Freedom, and the Rule of Law. In *You have to admit it's getting better: From economic prosperity to environmental quality*, ed. Terry L. Anderson. Stanford, Calif.: Hoover Institution Press.

Pacala, Stephen W., George C. Hurtt, David Baker, Philippe Peylin, Richard A. Houghton, Richard A. Birdsey, Linda Heath, Eric T. Sundquist, R. F. Stallard, Philippe Ciais, Paul Moorcroft, John P. Caspersen, Elena Shevliakova, Berrien Moore, Gundolf Kohlmaier, Elisabeth Holland, M. Gloor, Mark E. Harmon, Song-Miao Fan, Jorge L. Sarmiento, Christine L. Goodale, David Schimel, Christopher B. Field. 2001. Consistent land- and atmosphere-based U.S. carbon sink estimates. *Science* 292 (June 22): 2316–20.

Post, Wilfred M., and Kyung C. Kwon. 2000. Soil carbon sequestration and land-use change: Processes and potential. *Global Change Biology* 6 (3): 317–27.

Preuss, Paul. 2001. Climate change scenarios compel studies of ocean carbon storage. *Science Beat*, February 1. Berkeley, Calif.: Ernest Orlando Lawrence Berkeley National Laboratory. Online: http://www.lbl.gov/ Science-Articles/Archive/sea-carb-bish.html.

Simon, Julian L. 1995. *The state of humanity* Malden, Mass.: Blackwell Publishers.

———. 1999. *Hoodwinking the nation*. New Brunswick, N.J.: Transaction Press.

U.S. Department of Agriculture. 2001. Published estimates database. National Agriculture Statistics Service (NAAS). Online: http://www.nass.usda .gov:81/ipedb/.

U.S. Department of Agriculture, Natural Resources Conservation Service. 2000. *1997 National Resources Inventory (Revised December 2000)*. Online: http://www.nrcs.usda.gov/technical/NRI/1997/summary_report/index.html.

U.S. Department of Commerce, Bureau of Economic Affairs. Current-dollar and "real GDP." Online: http://www.bea.doc.gov/bea/dn1.htm.

U.S. Department of Energy. 1999. Carbon sequestration: Research and development. Online: http://www.fe.doe.gov/coal_power/sequestration/reports/rd/index.shtml.

———. 2001. Annual energy review 2000. Online: http://www.eia.doe.gov/emeu/aer/.

U.S. Department of Energy, Energy Information Administration. Energy consumption by sector, 1949–2000. Online: http://www.eia.doe.gov/emeu/aer/txt/ptb0201a.html.

U.S. Department of Energy and U.S. Environmental Protection Agency. 2000. Carbon dioxide emissions from the generation of electric power in the United States. Online: http://www.eia.doe.gov/cneaf/electricity/page/co2_report/co2emiss.pdf.

U.S. Environmental Protection Agency. 2000. Inventory of U.S. greenhouse gas emissions and sinks: 1990–1998. EPA 236-R-00-001. Office of Atmospheric Programs. Online http://www.epa.gov/globalwarming/publications/emissions/us2000/index.html.

———. 2001. Municipal solid waste in the United States: 1999 facts and figures. EPA-530-R-01-014. Online: http://www.epa.gov/epaoswer/non-hw/muncpl/pubs/mswfinal.pdf.

U.S. Fish and Wildlife Service. 2001. Report to Congress on the status and trends of wetlands in the conterminous United States 1986 to 1997. Online: http://wetlands.fws.gov/bha/SandT/SandTReport.html.

Utt, Joshua A., W. Walker Hunter, and Robert E. McCormick. 2002. Assessing the relation between net carbon emissions and income—Some basic information. Working Paper WP02-06. Bozeman, Mont.: PERC.

Index

acid rain, 2, 7–8; fear of, 25
AFBF. *See* American Farm Bureau
  Federation
Africa; caloric intake in, 45n16;
  deforestation in, 92, 98–99; poverty in,
  68. *See also* sub-Saharan countries
agricultural commerce, trade and, 123
agricultural production, carbon
  sequestration and, 186–87; human well-
  being and, 150; meteorological conditions
  and, 17; population growth and, 148–59
agricultural yields, xviii, 15, 34, 72, 74
agriculture, carbon emissions, and, 177–78
AIDS, 61, 70–71, 75, 76, 129
air pollution, 103n4; criteria for, 99; GDP
  and, 93; in London, 21; measurement of,
  102–3n3; in *The Skeptical
  Environmentalist,* 37–38
air quality, xiv, xv, xix, 104n5;
  environmental Kuznets curve and, 87–90,
  93–94, 98, 101, 102; GDP and, 88–89;
  improvement of, 95; political power and,
  102; trade and, 120, 123–24
alcoholism, in Russia, 60

Aldrich, Mark, 9–10, 45n8
American Farm Bureau Federation
  (AFBF), 26, 29
Antweiler, Werner, 120, 123, 137
appropriation, institutional quality and, 97
arable land, 14
Argentina, forests in, 11
Asia, deforestation in, 92, 98–99; poverty
  in, 68
Asimov, Isaac, on Easter Island, 18–19
Ausubel, J. H., 63

Bandopadhyay, Sushenjit, 89, 104n6
Baron, Sal, 30
Barro, Robert, 159
Bates, J. M., 95–96, 97
Bayer, Joseph, 41
Becker, Gary, 159
BERI. *See* Business Environmental Risk
  Intelligence
Bhagwati, Jagdish, 121, 127, 129, 130
Bhattarai, Madhusudan, 98; findings on
  institutional quality of, xvii

.